Forgotten Confederates

Library of Congress Cataloging-in-Publication Data

Forgotten Confederates
compiled & edited by
Charles Kelly Barrow, J. H. Segars & R. B. Rosenburg
Includes bibliographical references and index

ISBN 0-9631963-6-9 (paperback)
ISBN 0-9631963-6-8 (casebound)

95-071119

CIP

Forgotten Confederates

An Anthology About Black Southerners

Compiled & Edited
by
Charles Kelly Barrow, J. H. Segars, & R. B. Rosenburg

Journal of Confederate History Series
VOL. XIV

Southern Heritage Press
Post Office Box 347163
Atlanta, GA 30334

The whole subject of the 'Negro's Civil War' is perhaps vastly more complex, and perhaps more ambiguous or paradoxical, than most of us realized.

Robert F. Durden
The Gray and The Black

Contents

★ BLACK SOUTHERNERS IN GRAY? ★

THERE IS A CONTINUING NEED FOR HISTORIANS TO FOCUS ON certain aspects of American history which either have been neglected, overlooked, or altogether forgotten. Through closer examinations of these subordinated and relatively obscure subjects, one can obtain a clearer view and a more complete and accurate rendering of the past than previously known. In the current age of multiculturalism, the focus is broadening to encompass the study of the participation of blacks in all of the nation's wars, particularly the War Between the States, 1861-1865. The Union's 54th Massachusetts Infantry regiment received national attention in recent depictions in journals, books, and the feature film *Glory*. Americans' eyes were opened: The brave men of the 54th received recognition long overdue. Ironically, the story of these troops was not really new, but existed for many years in antiquarian books and seldom-consulted archival records. Moreover, the stories of other black troops are still waiting to be rediscovered by those of the present generation.

To one extent or the other, historians find that men and women of color were involved in all of America's wars. If this finding is indeed the case, then a most provocative and unsettling question arises: Could black Southerners also have supported the war efforts of the Confederate States of America? If so, why? For students schooled in the modern interpretations of the American Civil War, the idea of slaves or free blacks supporting the Southern Confederacy seems entirely improbable if not ludicrous. In addition, some would question the ultimate loyalty of "black Confederates," while others, conceding that such support did take place, point out that these occurrences should be viewed as nothing more than insignificant footnotes to history.

Americans continue to have difficulty in comprehending and evaluating the complexities of this terrible war. The twentieth century mind seems unable to grasp an understanding of the black Confederate. As Edward Smith, Dean of Minority Affairs and Professor of History at American University, remarked in the August 1991 edition of *The Civil War News*: "to admit that blacks actually fought for a cause which in the minds of many 20th century Americans now stands exclusively for slavery and oppression is unacceptable to many in the country concerned with only politics and not with the realities of historical record."

To date, only a small number of works has appeared in print on this subject; an amazing phenomenon, when one considers that some Civil War topics are explored, literally, hundreds and thousands of times. Some of the most notable publications include: Bell I. Wiley's *Southern Negroes, 1861-1865;* Robert F. Durden's *The Gray and The Black: The Confederate Debate on Emancipation;* and Hubert C. Blackerby's *Blacks in Blue and Gray: Afro-American Service in the Civil War.* But the lack of published books about black Confederates does not mean that there is a shortage of research material available. Reliable information may be obtained from a broad spectrum of sources found in libraries, state archives, historical societies, and private collections.

The idea for this study originated with Charles Kelly Barrow, a historical researcher with a longterm interest in black Confederates. To supplement his research, Barrow called upon the readership of the *Confederate Veteran,* the official magazine of the Sons of Confederate Veterans, to submit information about blacks loyal to the South. For more than five years, scores of S.C.V. members, historians, and students of the war responded with a large, diverse mixture of material, comprised of the following: archival records, pension applications, official reports, personal letters, photographs, veteran reminiscences, military records, family narratives, book excerpts, newspaper articles, journal selections, and published writings of the past and present. Many of the respondents sent nothing more than letters of encouragement, wanting to know when the book would become available. Barrow discovered that he was not alone in his interest in this subject.

Analyzing, editing, and compiling the broad assortment of research material proved to be a formidable challenge. Taken as a whole, the material could have been categorized into a series of short excerpts, archival extracts, and listings. But, in order to explore the topic fully, it seemed necessary to include additional narrative. Aside from the eyewitness reports, newspaper accounts, archival records, and veteran statements, we believed that it was most important to include the perspective of Civil War veterans, such as Alabama Governor and Confederate General William C. Oates, Union soldier and African-American orator James T. Wilson, and Confederate private and Georgia author Henry W. Thomas. Selections are reprinted from the authoritative works of these men, as well as articles from the original *Confederate Veteran* magazine and Kent

State University's *Civil War History*. Contemporary scholarship has been provided by Professor C. W. Harper of North Carolina State University, Professor Jay Hoar of the University of Maine at Farmington, and historian Wayne Austerman. Others providing insight include Edward Raffetto and Charles Lunsford. A valuable selection is Gene Armistead's "Sources for the Study of Black Confederates," which serves as an annotated bibliography for this work.

As a whole, this volume can pretend to be nothing more than what it is: an anthology of historical documents and accounts about black Southerners who served on the side of the Confederacy, based upon a variety of sources. Although neither perfect nor complete, the work provides a beginning (or continuation) for those interested in this fascinating and controversial aspect of American history. Regardless of the amount of research material available or the level of scholarship applied, there never will be total agreement over the role of African-Americans supporting the Confederacy or the exact number serving within southern military units. Nevertheless, if one considers the most conservative estimates of 50,000 to 60,000, then the numbers are significant as compared to the estimated figures for white men in the Confederate ranks, 600,000 to 1,000,000 (depending on which side did the counting). As Professor Leonard Haynes of Southern University recently put it: "When you eliminate the black Confederate soldier, you've eliminated the history of the South."

Perhaps the greatest debate is whether the term "soldier" can be properly applied to these black men (and women) who served as servants, bodyguards, nurses, cooks, scouts, barbers, teamsters, and construction laborers, and who in many cases "joined the fight" without official governmental sanction. This point could be well argued either way. The *American Heritage Dictionary* defines a soldier as "one who serves in an army; an enlisted person or a non-commissioned officer; and an active loyal and militant follower." By this definition, with the exception of "proper enlistment," the designation "black Confederates" might qualify; though in some cases they were carried on official rolls, even though the authorization for official black companies was not approved by the Confederate Congress and signed into law by President Davis until near the end of the war, on March 18, 1865. Moreover, if proper enlistment is a definitive criterion, then thousands of white men who served in state and local militia units would not qualify as soldiers either.

There is much irony to be found in the story of black Confederates. Men of color served within Confederate companies, while their Union counterparts were separated from white troops. The Confederate government authorized equal pay for musicians, many of whom were black. And free men of color and some servants received compensation for their war efforts. Dr. Richard Rollins, editor of *Black Southerners in Gray: Essays on Afro-Americans in Confederate Armies* (Volume XI of the *Journal of Confederate History Series*), found that twenty-five percent of the Confederate Ordinance Department consisted of black men and that early in the war several black militia units were raised in Louisiana and Alabama. Most ironic of all, Rollins discovered several monuments in the South dedicated to the service of African-Americans loyal to the Confederacy, while few are in the North. Moreover, Prof. Ervin L. Jordan, Jr., author of *Black Confederates and Afro-Yankees in Civil War Virginia*, writes:

> Numerous black Virginians served with Confederate forces as soldiers, sailors, teamsters, spies, and hospital personnel. For example, blacks joined the Confederate navy but by law a ship's crew was not to be more than one-twentieth black, [though] in February 1865 Secretary of the Navy Stephen R. Mallory admitted his navy's need of an additional 1,150 black seamen.
>
> I know of black Confederate sharpshooters who saw combat during the 1862 Seven Days Campaign and [of] the existence of black companies [which] organized and drilled in Richmond during March-April 1865. Integrated companies of black and white hospital workers fought against the Union army in the Petersburg trenches during March 1865. There were several recruitment campaigns and charity balls held in Virginia on behalf of black soldiers and special camps of instruction were established to train them. During March 1865 fully-armed black Confederate soldiers were seen in Richmond; one of the last Confederate prisoners at Point Lookout was described as a 'Negro reb.'

The bonds between southern families and their African-American allies are not easily understood, especially by those unfamiliar with the region's history. In many instances deep devotion and affection transcended the master-slave relationship and was not destroyed by the divisive wedge of Federal reconstruction. The love of homeland, as well as a traditional Christian upbringing, might partially explain why men and women of color could support the Southern Confederacy, even at the expense of immediate emancipation. Suffice it to say, black Confederates were not fighting for their own enslavement but sincerely believed that their ultimate freedom, prosperity, and destiny lay south of the Mason-Dixon line.

Not unlike their fellow Southerners engaged in the most tragic of wars, black Confederates were a bold and adventurous lot. Although racial inequality and social injustice are also a part of southern history, so is the historic fidelity and commonality shared by many different races and creeds in the South. The story of black Confederates should not be forgotten.

J. H. Segars

VETERANS POSE FOR A PHOTOGRAPH IN VIDALIA, GEORGIA (*ca.* 1900).
Courtesy Ken W. Smith

★ BLACK LOYALTY UNDER THE CONFEDERACY ★

CHARLES W. HARPER

SCHOLARS OF SOUTHERN HISTORY LARGELY HAVE AVOIDED THE task of linking African-Americans to the Confederate States war effort. That effort is conceded to have been a thrust toward southern independence, with a resulting continuance of enslavement. It is undoubtedly disturbing and illogical to some people that black Southerners could directly lend support to this effort.

Many have written to affirm the disloyalty of southern blacks to the Confederate cause and their homeland. In an article in *The Journal of Negro History*, "Slave Disloyalty Under the Confederacy" (1938), Harvey Wish argued that "thousands of slaves deserted to Union forces," while admitting that "the extent of slave disloyalty can only be inferred rather than stated with precision." In a study published thirty years later, James H. Brewer suggested that blacks supported a regime committed to their continued subjugation because they were "corroded by degradation and psychologically disabled by oppression." At the same time, Brewer offered tangible evidence of widespread black support to the southern war effort.[1]

In "The Unlikely Story of Blacks Who Were Loyal to Dixie," published in *Smithsonian*, J. K. Obatala offered that "the vision of the devoted slave, working loyally for his master's cause, is largely myth." However, Obatala conceded that there were outstanding and memorable instances of black patriotism among slaves and free men of color. Blacks were not merely passive participants in the southern cause, he noted, but were serving to protect their homes. Indeed, Obatala granted that the "Rebel black seems to have had at least a primitive, instinctive feeling that his fortunes were tied inextricably to those of the South: that he was a Southerner."

Joseph T. Wilson, a black veteran of a Federal regiment, apologized for the Confederate support of his brethren. Writing *The Black Phalanx: A History of the Negro Soldiers of the United States* (1890), Wilson maintained that blacks were induced to support the

---

The late Charles W. Harper was a professor at North Carolina State University, Raleigh, for nearly twenty-five years.

[1] *The Confederate Negro: Virginia's Craftsmen and Military Laborers* (1969).

Confederacy through fear or desire for personal gain. He suggested that refusal to join the southern cause would have invited torture, if not massacre. Thomas Morris Chester, a black war correspondent of the period, averred that "it must not be supposed that the blacks are to a man loyal to the old flag." He contended that the hesitating policy of the Lincoln government to enlist the aid of blacks, coupled with the "terrible recollection that fugitive slaves were returned by Union officers and that the belief that Yankees would sell them to Cuba induced many southern blacks to cling to the cause of the South under protest."[2]

Regardless of attempts to explain away black support or to camouflage or to ignore black efforts in behalf of the Confederacy, there is ample evidence suggesting that thousands of black Southerners voluntarily supported the Confederate cause, ignoring an offer of Federal freedom and, when allowed to do so, took up arms to defend Dixie.

Before and after the outbreak of hostilities in 1861, blacks were among the first Southerners to offer their services to the Confederacy. Local authorities throughout the South allowed the enlistment of free men of color for military service before such action had been taken by the Confederate government.[3] Accounts of black units organized for Confederate military services are found in George W. Williams, *A History of the Negro Troops in the War of the Rebellion, 1864-1865*, published in 1888. Horace Greeley wrote after the war: "For more than two years [before the Lincoln government authorized the use of black troops], Negroes had been extensively employed in belligerent operations by the Confederacy."

North Carolina newspapers of the era liberally illustrate efforts of southern free blacks in behalf of their state and the Confederacy. In the summer of 1861, *The Winston Salem People's Press* reported "Fifteen free men of color left [Salisbury, N. C.] Monday morning for the mouth of the Cape Fear, volunteers for the service of the State. They were in fine spirits and each wore a placard on his hat bearing the inscription, 'We will die by the South.' " On March 12, 1862, Stephen D. Collins and D. F. Edmond requested the consent of North

---

[2]R. J. Blackett, ed., *Thomas Morris Chester. Black Civil War Correspondent, His Dispatches from the Virginia Front* (1989).

[3]Charles H. Wesley, "The Employment of Negroes as Soldiers in the Confederate Army," *The Journal of Negro History* (July, 1919).

Carolina Governor John W. Ellis to support the State and Confederacy through military enlistments, having "been very strongly solicited by [their] neighbors, friends, and citizens to raise a company of free mulatives as there is so many near . . . that is willing to turn out in behalf of our homes and friends," adding: "There is a small place in about 10 miles of [Florisville, N. C.] called Scuffletown settled with free mulattos. There can easily be three full companies raised in that place. They say they are willing to raise arms against our Yankee foe and guard our coast."[4] On June 15, 1861, T. J. Minns, of Fayetteville, North Carolina, wrote Ellis: "[I] can raise a company of from fifty to one hundred able bodies mulattos or free men of color to serve the Southern Confederacy," while in New Bern, North Carolina, "fifteen or twenty more free Negroes came forward and volunteered their services as laborers or in defense of the city."[5]

Blacks in neighboring states joined their brethren in North Carolina in offering their services in defense of their state and to the Confederacy. According to the *Richmond Dispatch*, about fifty-three blacks in Amelia County, Virginia, offered themselves "to the government for any service."[6] That same newspaper reported that two hundred Petersburg, Virginia, free blacks offered to do any work assigned to them "either to fight under white officers, dig ditches, or anything that could show their desire to serve old Virginia."

One student of black Confederates noted the enlistment in a company of seventy free blacks pledged to defend the state, as well as black citizens of Petersburg, Virginia, who volunteered to help construct fortifications at Norfolk and who held a mass rally in the courthouse square to demonstrate their enthusiasm for the cause. Former Mayor John Dodson presented them a Confederate flag. The group's spokesman accepted the flag, replying, "We are willing to aid Virginia's cause to the utmost of our ability."[7]

Bowman Seals, a free man of color in Barbour County, Alabama, wrote Jefferson Davis on March 27, 1861, to volunteer his services to the Confederacy. He was convinced that if the North won the war

---

[4]Henry Toole Clark Papers, North Carolina Department of Archives and History, Raleigh.

[5]*New Bern Progress*, quoted in the *Greensborough* (N.C.) *Patriot*, Apr. 25, 1861.

[6]Quoted in the *Greensborough* (N.C.) *Patriot*, May 7, 1861.

[7]Wayne R. Austerman, "Virginia's Black Confederates," *Civil War Quarterly* (March 1987).

"the best poor man's country in the world will very soon be inevitably converted into a land of the extremist want and misery."[8]

Significantly, Frederick Douglass, escaped slave and abolitionist, observed in the fall of 1861:

> There are at the present moment, many colored men in the Confederate Army doing duty not only as cooks, servants, and laborers, but as real soldiers, having musket on their shoulders and bullets in their pockets, ready to shoot down loyal troops and do all that soldiers may do to destroy the Federal government and build up that of the traitors and rebels.[9]

Writing in 1919, Charles H. Wesley averred that to the majority of the blacks (nay, to most Southerners) the invading Northern Armies were ruthlessly attacking independent States, invading their beloved homeland and trampling upon all that Southerners held dear. To Wesley, blacks not only were loyal in remaining home and doing their duty but also in offering themselves for actual service in the Confederate army. Believing their land invaded by hostile foes, blacks were more than willing under the guidance of misguided Southerners to offer themselves for the service of actual warfare.[10]

When secession and war came to the South, hundreds if not thousands of free men of color were eager to join the southern colors, voluntarily. Yet they never were allowed to enlist in the Confederate Army, though many enlisted in state militias and home guard units. Moreover, there is no evidence that they took part as a large group in any major military engagement.

In the first year of the war, large numbers of slaves were received into the service of Confederate laboring units. The extent to which they entered state or Confederate service in some form or the other depended upon the consent of their masters. Blacks were employed substantially in building redoubts and fortifications, raising crops and casting cannons, and as teamsters, locomotive firemen, and hospital

---

[8]*Clayton* (Ala.) *Banner*, Apr. 18, 1861. See also Lynda L. Crist, ed., *The Papers of Jefferson Davis* 7: 82.

[9]Quoted in Dudley Taylor Cornish, *The Sable Arm: Negro Troops in the Union Army, 1861-1865* (1956).

[10]"The Employment of Negroes in the Confederate Army," *Journal of Negro History* 4 (1919): 239-53.

THE CONSTRUCTION OF CONFEDERATE FORTIFICATIONS.
Courtesy Arthur Shilstone & Smithsonian Magazine

nurses. The myriad of contributions on the southern home front are well known and documented.

In a speech in Raleigh, North Carolina, after the war, Dr. Daniel Harney Hill, son of the Confederate general, gave credit to the support of blacks to the southern cause. He remarked:

> Our people ought never to forget the fidelity of the Negroes during those defenseless days. With the doors of freedom often open for them, with opportunities for lawlessness during the absence of their owners, with a growing knowledge that the success of the Confederate Army would mean a continuance of their slavery, at least for a time, the Negroes, for the most part, refused to sever the ties that bound theirs to white families and continued their daily duties. In attendance on their masters in the field, in moving them from the field when they were wounded, in bringing home the bodies of their slain, in secreting and caring for family treasures, in watching over family interests, and in

> other ways, hundreds of Negroes displayed a noble fidelity that should always be remembered![11]

Black Southerners did more than tender their services. They also shared their material wealth with the Confederacy, further indicating direct and free volunteer support of the South's war effort. Black enthusiasm emerged during the early months of the war and remained a valuable resource for the Confederates. In Alabama blacks brought sixty dollars' worth of watermelons to Montgomery for soldiers.[12] In North Carolina a black servant reportedly came to his master and insisted that he accept his savings of one hundred dollars to help equip volunteers.[13] Similar propositions were made by both bond and free blacks through the whole of Virginia. In 1863, Henry Jones, a citizen of Clarksville, Virginia, placed at the disposal of the Confederate treasury $465 in gold.[14]

Some black Southerners used their artistic talents to generate funds for the Confederacy. J. K. Obatala discovered that a group in Charleston, South Carolina, called the "Confederate Ethiopian Serenaders," turned over the proceeds from one of their concerts to help finance the production of gunboats and munitions. According to E. Merton Coulter, it was customary for blacks to hold balls and donate money to aid patriotic causes and to support soldiers' families. Gary B. Mills found that the Louisiana Cane River Creoles of color publicly favored the Confederacy throughout the conflict. They deprived themselves and their families to help maintain Confederate forces.[15]

One North Carolina newspaper reported that blacks in Louisburg, Virginia, at their own suggestion, gave a feast to Confederate soldiers in the area. This feast occurred less than two months before Appomattox. Eighteen black citizens of Savannah, Georgia, subscribed the sum of ninety dollars for the relief of Georgia soldiers fighting in Virginia. Blacks presented to Jordan's Georgia regiment seventy-two pairs of socks. In New Bern, North Carolina, blacks

---

[11]Georgia Hicks Papers, North Carolina Department of Archives and History, Raleigh.

[12]*Charlotte Daily Bulletin*, Aug. 8, 1862.

[13]*Greensborough* (N.C.) *Patriot*, May 7, 1861.

[14]*Charlotte Western Democrat*, Aug. 25, 1863; *Fayetteville*, (N.C.) *Observer*, Aug. 17, 1863.

[15]*The Forgotten People: Cane River's Creoles of Color* (1977).

contributed two thousand pounds of scrap metal to be melted and cast into cannon balls.[16]

Numerous incidents during the war, when slaves (contraband) taken by Union forces escaped or returned to their homes, are also indications of fidelity to masters, to the state or to the Confederacy. Certainly this statement is not without its detractors and skeptics. Harvey Wish has argued that slaves did not rise up and slaughter their masters during the war out of loyalty but civilized restraint. It was not unusual for servants of the class working in and around the plantation mansion, in close proximity to the white owner, to become very much attached to the white family and very faithful. It was not uncommonforthem to consider themselves as constituting part of the master's family. The antebellum South was a home worth fighting for and living in for the majority of blacks who were born and lived there.[17]

A number of black Southerners were forcefully carried off by the Union Army, but later sought their own release. In March 1865 a squad of Union cavalry carried off nineteen black men from Monroe, North Carolina. Thirteen of these men escaped the night of their capture and returned to their homes.[18] The January 31, 1862, edition of the *Winston Salem People's Press* contains several accounts of blacks taken by the Union army who later escaped and returned to their masters. Writing to his wife from Camden, South Carolina, on February 26, 1865, Thomas J. Myers, a lieutenant with Sherman's army complained:

> The d_ _ _ _d niggers, as a general rule preferred to stay at home particularly when they found out that we only wanted the able bodied men (and to tell you the truth the youngest and best looking women). Sometimes we took off whole families and plantation of niggers, by way of repaying some influential secessionists.[19]

---

[16] *Fayetteville* (N.C.) *Observer*, Feb. 27, 1865; *Asheville* (N.C.) *News*, Nov. 20, 1862; *Milledgeville* (Ga.) *Union*, quoted in *Charlotte Daily Bulletin*, Apr. 11, 1862; *New Bern Weekly Progress*, May 25, 1861.

[17] Wish, "Slave Disloyalty Under the Confederacy," (1938). See also C. W. Harper, "House Servants and Field Hands: Fragmentation in the Antebellum Slave Community," *North Carolina Historical Review* (1978).

[18] *Raleigh* (N.C.) *Daily Conservative*, Mar. 21, 1865.

[19] Thomas J. Myers Papers, North Carolina Department of Archives and History, Raleigh.

Union troops in the neighborhood of Shepardstown, [West] Virginia, carried off several black men to Maryland. Upon being told that they were free, they asked to return to their masters, on account of the fact that their wives and children were still in Virginia. Four of the men from Clark, Virginia, enjoyed freedom in Pennsylvania before voluntarily returning home.[20]

Roben Hale Strong found that "sometimes the nigs were loyal to their masters. Then neither coaxing nor threats would induce them to tell where things were hidden."[21] In Virginia two servants remained at Norfolk when that city was captured by Union forces. Retaining possession of their master's carriage and horse, they made their escape to Suffolk and then to Charlotte. These men could have converted the carriage and horse to cash and claimed their freedom; instead, they elected to rejoin their master in the Confederacy.[22]

It would be naive to suggest that blacks failed to flee slavery in numbers. The evidence is to the contrary. James M. McPherson has estimated that approximately 500,000 slaves came within Union lines during the war. In 1860 the black population of the Confederacy was 3.5 million. Therefore, it is safe to say, for whatever reason, the majority of slaves did not flee to Union lines. Moreover, it is probable that many of those who did would have returned to the Confederacy if allowed to do so by United States authorities.[23]

There are numerous cases where blacks who ran away voluntarily returned to their homes and masters or sought to do so. Thirty-four of forty blacks of Culpeper County, Virginia, who ran off returned to their former homes and "expressed themselves as entirely satisfied with their sojourn among the Yankees."[24] The *Raleigh Standard* of January 11, 1862, reported that blacks "continue to run off to the Yankees in Virginia but when they get a chance to leave they at once return to their masters." After Union troops raided Little River, North Carolina, the *Wilmington Journal* indicated that blacks

---

[20] *Winchester* (VA) *Republican*, quoted in the *Raleigh* (N.C.) *Standard*, Jan. 22, 1862.

[21] Ashley Halsey, ed., "A Yankee Private's Civil War," (1961).

[22] *Charlotte Daily Bulletin*, May 24, 1862.

[23] *The Negro's Civil War: How American Negroes Felt and Acted During the War of the Union* (1965).

[24] *Richmond Dispatch*, quoted in *Fayetteville* (N.C.) *Observer*, Sept. 1, 1862.

refused to accompany them upon their departure, "many should have gone off, but did not."[25]

It is interesting to note that Northern newspapers seemed somewhat perplexed at the lack of enthusiasm exhibited by blacks when Union forces appeared. The reaction by the *Providence* (R. I.) *Post* was typical:

> Negroes as a mass have shown no friendship to the Union--have neither sought to achieve their liberty nor to subdue their masters. The few thousands who have come into our lines to live at the expense of the whites seek rather a life of laziness than self-dependence. Their sympathies are with the rebels.... The truth is that there never was a greater humbling than the talk about Negro loyalty. Abolition has asserted it from the beginning of the war, but every fact of the times proves it is a mere assertion.[26]

This sentiment was echoed in 1862 by *Blackwood's Magazine* of England. In order to "judge of ourselves what condition of things was in the land of Dixie," the magazine had sent to the Confederacy Sir James Ferguson, who, upon the termination of his southern trip, observed:

> It is undoubtedly true that, not withstanding the strenuous efforts of abolitionists, the Negroes bear the yoke [slavery] cheerfully and heartily join their fortunes to those of their masters in the great struggle in which they are now engaged.[27]

The New York *Journal of Commerce* worried in 1862 that few blacks had come into the Union at Port Royal, Virginia. The number recorded by the newspaper did not exceed 350. Furthermore,

> No indication has been given of any desire to accept liberty as a permanency. Their attachment to their masters and the families to which they belong does not seem to be diminished and there are large numbers probably thousands of them in the neighborhood who have not come into the fort at all.[28]

---

[25]*Wilmington Journal,* May 28, 1862.
[26]*Asheville* (N.C.) *News,* July 31, 1862.
[27]*Greensborough* (N.C.) *Patriot,* Feb. 6, 1862.
[28]Quoted in *New Bern Weekly Progress,* Sept. 7, 1861; *Winston Salem People's Press,* Jan. 3, 1862.

Early in the war some black Southerners found that they did not better their material lot substantially by escaping to Union army camps. According to the *Macon* (Ga.) *Telegraph*, blacks as a general rule came to prefer to remain with their masters. In addition, blacks within Union lines advised their fellow blacks that they "would not profit by a change of masters and [added tales] of suffering, destitution and mortality among Negroes in the rear."[29]

This assertion is substantiated in part by U.S. Congressman Wickliffe of Kentucky, who disclosed in May 1862 that

> slaves who have been taken [at Port Royal] mostly desire to return to their masters, and are prohibited from doing so by the military authorities governing them. I have the assurance that when some of the slaves had attempted to leave the camp for the purpose of getting back to their masters, they were fired on by the sentinels acting under the orders of their superior officers.[30]

The Washington correspondent of the *New York Express* added:

> Hundreds of them have had already quite enough of liberty and abolition philanthropy. They would gladly return now to their masters and mistresses but have no power to do so, and, indeed, are not permitted any opportunity to carry such desire into effect.[31]

Reporting from Union-held New Bern, North Carolina, a correspondent of the *New York Tribune* gave the following assessment of the treatment of blacks in that area in October 1862:

> The situation of the poor, unhappy blacks . . . is such as should excite the sympathy of every Christian man. I am sorry to say that they are treated with great sternness and severity amounting to positive cruelty, by our own soldiers who seem to regard them as hardly better than beasts. Not a few of our officers conduct themselves in the most unfeeling manner toward these unfortunate creatures and are in fact. . . expressing their hatred and contempt for the 'd- - - -d nigger.'[32]

29Quoted in the *Raleigh Daily Conservative*, June 6, 1864.
30*Fayetteville Observer*, May 26, 1862.
31 Quoted in *Asheville News*, Nov. 20, 1862.
32Quoted in the *Charlotte Daily Bulletin*, Nov. 13, 1862.

The *Boston Courier* shuddered "at the awful condition of the Negroes . . . and justice is outraged by the sending them away from their homes. They are huddled together in very foul places, suffering and dying from exposure and disease."[33]

Noted historian John Hope Franklin recognized the suffering and death among blacks in Union camps and placed the mortality rate at twenty-five percent. As Elizabeth Keckley, a devoted companion and seamstress to Mary Todd Lincoln in the White House during the four years of the Lincoln presidency, observed in her autobiography:

> The emancipated slaves, in coming north, left old associations behind them, and the love for the past was so strong that they could find [little] beauty in the new life so suddenly opened to them. Thousands of the disappointed huddled together in camps, fretted and pined like children for the 'good old times.' In visiting them . . . they would crowd around me with pitiful stories of distress. Often I heard them declare that they would rather go back to slavery in the South and be with their old masters than to enjoy the freedom of the north. I believe they were sincere in these declarations.[34]

Indeed, a reporter with the *Boston Courier* felt "they all want to go home and if the government would allow it, they would all go back."[35]

Possibly the most severe test of fidelity and loyalty during the war came to personal servants of white Southerners. No class of servants had such excellent opportunities to desert or to evidence disloyalty. Yet this class almost never deserted. Black Confederates followed their masters to war, worked as teamsters, laborers, foragers and cooks in the Confederate army, and did yeoman service, shouldering arms and burning gunpowder in combat, and when captured entered Yankee prisons as prisoners of war. In *The Life of Johnny Reb: The Common Soldier of the Confederacy* (1943), Bell Wiley argued that the black Confederates' relation to the southern fighting force was so vital and so intimate as to merit consideration as part of the Confederate army. In his *Reminiscences of the Civil War* (1904), Confederate General John B. Gordon wrote that "Negroes seemed to be as thoroughly imbued with the feeling which prevailed in the

---

33 Quoted in the *Greensborough Patriot*, Apr. 16, 1863.
34 *Behind the Scenes: Thirty Years a Slave and Four Years in the White House.*
35 Quoted in the *Asheville News*, Apr. 16, 1863.

Confederate ranks as were the soldiers themselves and spoke with as much pride of Confederate achievement."

Many black Southerners thought of themselves as Confederates. As a former slave who was just a child in 1861 put it: "Us war Confederates all the while . . . cause ole Marse was and Marse Jeff woulda fit 'em too and me with him iffen we had been old enough."[36] Another black Rebel "went to fight the Yankees," recalling afterward that "we wan't beaten, we wuz starved Out." There also is the legend from Virginia of "Charlie," who shook his fist at the Yankee invaders and shouted, "Don't you know dis is de Tabb Place? Ain't you never heard of States rights? Git on off wid you."[37]

Certainly black service in the Confederate army consisted of more than body servants accompanying their masters to war. This assertion is clearly revealed by Moses of Virginia, who upon being captured addressed his captors: "I had as much right to fight for my native state as you had to fight for your'n, and a blame sight more right than you furiners, what's got no homes."[38] Revealed is an attachment to home and hearth, an indication that Moses saw Virginia as his native state worth defending against an outside force. This same attitude is evident in a letter from a Georgia family nurse writing to her master away to war.

> Do if you come in contact with any of those heartless Yankees, give them a few shots of a bombshell and clear them from our coasts. They never gave us our home and they have no right to it. Our soldiers may have a long fight, but I hope they will fight, and watch, and pray, and never give up the field.[39]

Mariah Bowens, a free mulatto servant of Winton, North Carolina, wrote the following on February 19, 1862, to a free black in care of Capt. John Randolph, New Bern, North Carolina:

> The Federals came in and walked about some two or three hours and finally left it. Some people think that we are in a very dangerous predicament, others think we are safe. The majority of the people of

---

[36] B.A. Bothin, ed., *Lay My Burden Down: A Folk History of Slavery* (1945).

[37] Federal Writers' Program of the Work Progress Administration in the State of Virginia, comp., "The Negro in Virginia," (1940).

[38] H. C. Blackerly, *Blacks in Blue and Gray: Afro-American Service in the Civil War* (1979).

[39] *Savannah News* quoted in the *Charlotte Daily Bulletin*, Nov. 6, 1862.

> this place think their intentions are to reach Norfolk and Weldon. I hope that they will not be successful, indeed I think they will not for I am certain that God is on our side and that his strong arm will protect our weak Confederacy. You need not have any fears as to my safety for I will not suffer the vandals to disturb me. I will not even give them a chance.

From the earliest days of the war to Appomattox, black Rebels appeared in combat with Confederate forces. In June 1861 Union General Benjamin Butler at Fortress Monroe, Virginia, received information of southern troops at Big Bethel Church, about thirteen miles from Yorktown. Butler organized a force with instructions to drive back the Rebels and to destroy their camp. In the ensuing firefight, Maj. Theodore Winthrop, leading Vermont and Massachusetts troops against the First North Carolina Regiment (later "Bethel Regiment"), was shot through the heart, possibly the first Union officer to lose his life in combat. Of some four North Carolina soldiers firing at Major Winthrop, one was black, the servant of Captain Ashe, Company D. Captain Ashe claimed his servant fired the fatal shot. Certainly the servant, Sam, was in the ranks expending ammunition in an effort to fell Major Winthrop.[40]

Essie Matthews related the brief story of "Uncle Gus," who served in the Confederate army, first as a bodyguard, subsequently as a teamster, and at other times in the ranks.[41] Frazer Kirkland reminisced about the following incident which had occurred more than thirty years earlier:

> One of the best mornings' work done at Yorktown was that of reducing to a state of perfect inutility in this mundane sphere a rebel Negro rifleman, who, through his skill as a marksman, had done more injury to our men than any dozen of his white compeers, in the attempted labor of trimming off the complement of union sharp-shooters. His habit was to perch himself in a big tree and keeping himself hid behind the body, annoy the Union men by firing upon them.[42]

George Townsend, a "Yankee reporter" who may have been British, reported that the last gun discharged from Yorktown, as the

---

[40]Maj. Edward J. Hale, "The Bethel Regiment: The First NC Volunteers" in Walter Clark, ed., *Histories of the Several Regiments and Battalions from North Carolina in the Great War, 1861-65* (1901).

[41]*Aunt Phebe, Uncle Tom, and Others: Character Studies Among the Old Slaves of the South, Fifty Years After* (1915).

[42]*Reminiscences of the Blue and Gray '61-65, Embracing the Most Brilliant and Thrilling Short Stories of the Civil War* (1895).

Confederate army moved north, was said to have been fired by a Negro. Scouts of the First Vermont Infantry reported in August 1861 a Richmond Howitzer battery manned by blacks at New Market Bridge, Virginia. The regiment's commander, Col. J. L. Phelps, added with regard to the artillery being manned by blacks: "I think the report probably correct." In April 1861 a company of sixty free blacks marched into Richmond with a Confederate flag at the head of their column. Asking to join the repulse of the northern invader, they were sent home after being complimented for their show of southern patriotism.[43] Black Confederates had better luck joining southern ranks as individuals or as twos or threes rather than in large numbers.

George assisted in capturing guns used before Richmond during the Seven Days battles. He also accompanied the army into Pennsylvania, where his master insisted on his accepting his freedom and joining a settlement of free blacks near Gettysburg. George would have none of it. Later, dressed in gray, he was killed in action.

Union General George H. Gordon reported "many men from my command were killed, and strange stories bruited about of the precision and fire of a Negro marksman, a Rebel." Philip Thomas Tucker found at least one black servant-turned-warrior who stood in the ranks eager for the assault during the battle of Port Gibson.

During action at Crumpler's Bluff, Union forces there made a disconcerting discovery: they observed that black riflemen had played a conspicuous part in the fire that raked their gunboats. Ely Williamson, a local mulatto who was pilot on a Confederate steamer that took part in the battle of Roanoke Island, North Carolina, had his arm shattered from elbow to wrist.

There are numerous accounts of black participation in the battle of First Manassas in the summer of 1861. Black combatants shot, killed, and captured Union troops. Loyal slaves were said to have fought with outstanding bravery alongside their masters. These reports also provide testimony to the fidelity of black Rebels in combat. One black soldier was moving about the field when ordered to surrender by a Union officer. The Rebel replied, "No sir, you are my prisoner," while drawing a pistol and shooting the officer dead. He then secured the officer's sidearm and after the battle boasted loudly of having

---

43 Austerman, "Virginia's Black Confederates."

quieted at least one of "the stinkin' Yankees who cam here 'specting to whip us Southerners."[44] Another black Confederate who stood behind a tree allowed two Union soldiers to pass before shooting one in the shoulders, clubbing him with a pistol, while demanding the other to surrender. Both prisoners were marched into Confederate lines.[45] An Alabama officer's servant marched a Zouave into camp proclaiming, "Massa, here one of dese devils who been shooting at us, Suh."[46]

The efforts of Jack, servant of an officer of the Thirteenth Arkansas Regiment, stands out as an act of heroism. Jack fought beside his master during the heat of battle. He fell seriously wounded but refused to be evacuated and continued to fire at the enemy. He later died in a hospital of his wounds sustained in the ranks of the Confederate army.[47]

John Parker was one of four black men in an artillery battery at First Manassas. A *New York Times* correspondent with Grant's army in 1863 found a "rebel battery manned almost wholly by Negroes, a single white man or perhaps two directing operations."[48]

Angered at the loss of life at the hands of blacks at Manassas and somewhat disillusioned the northern *Exchange* editorialized:

> The war has dispelled one delusion of the abolitionists. The Negroes regard them as enemies instead of friends. No insurrection has occurred in the South--no important stampede of slaves has evinced their desire for freedom. On the contrary, they have jeered at and insulted our troops, heave readily enlisted in the rebel army and on Sunday, at Manassas, shot down our men with as much alacrity as if abolitionism had never existed.[49]

The *New York Tribune* reprinted a Union soldier's letter addressed to the *Indianapolis Star*, December 23, 1861, with the heading "Attack on Our Soldiers by Armed Negroes." The letter read, in part:

---

44 *Charlotte Western Democrat*, July 29, 1861.

45 *Montgomery Advertiser* quoted in *Salisbury Carolina Watchman*, Aug. 15, 1861; *Richmond Dispatch* quoted in *Fayetteville Observer*, July 29, 1861.

46 *Charlotte Western Democrat*, Aug. 6, 1861. This issue has several instances of blacks who captured Union troops at First Manassas.

47 *Memphis Avalanche* quoted in *Charlotte Western Democrat*, Dec. 31, 1861.

48 Obatala, "The Unlikely Story of Blacks Who Were Loyal to Dixie."

49 Quoted in *New Bern Weekly Press*, Aug. 13, 1861; *Charlotte Western Democrat*, Aug. 13, 1861.

> A body of seven hundred Negro infantry opened fire on our men, wounding two lieutenants and two privates. The wounded men testify positively that they were shot by Negroes, and that not less than seven hundred were present, armed with muskets. This is, indeed, a new feature in the war. We have heard of a regiment of Negroes at Manassas, and another at Memphis, and still another at New Orleans, but did not believe it till it came so near home and attacked our men.

The "attack" supposedly occurred at New Market Bridge, near Newport News, Virginia. Unfortunately, sources to verify the soldier's tale are nonexistent.

By 1862 large number of black Southerners were fully integrated into the Confederate army, as illustrated by Capt. Isaac W. Heysinger, a Marylander. Captain Heysinger observed the Army of Northern Virginia as it moved through Frederick, Maryland, toward an appointment at Sharpsburg.

> At four o'clock this morning the rebel army began to move from our town, Jackson's force taking the advance. The most liberal calculation could not have given them more than 64,000 men. Over 3,000 Negroes must be included in that number. These were clad in all kinds of uniforms, not only cast off or captured United States uniforms, but in coats with Southern buttons, State buttons, etc. They were shabby, but not shabbier or seedier looking than those worn by white men in the rebel ranks. Most of the Negroes had arms, rifles, muskets, sabers, bowie knives, dirks, etc. They were supplied, in many instances, with knapsacks, haversacks, canteens, etc., and were manifestly an integral portion of the Southern Confederacy Army. They were seen riding on horses and mules, driving wagons, riding on caissons, in ambulances, with the staff of generals, and promiscuously mixed up with all the rebel horde.[50]

During cavalry operations on the first Maryland campaign, from August 30 to September 18, 1862, Gen. J. E. B. Stuart sent Col. T. T. Munford and the Second Virginia Cavalry to Leesburg to capture a band of marauders and their leader, Means, which had infested and harassed the inhabitants of that area. Stuart reported: "In this engagement Edmund, a slave belonging to one of the men, charged with the regiment and shot Averhart one of the most notorious ruffians."

Capt. George Baylor of the Twelfth Virginia Cavalry recalled that Uncle John, one of his servants, "rendered himself very obnoxious

---

[50] *Antietam and the Maryland and Virginia Campaigns 1862* (1912).

to the Yankees by taking an active part in taking them over the Potomac river at Harper's Ferry and into a trap laid for them by a posse of our men." During the cavalry battle at Brandy Station, Virginia, in June 1863, Captain Baylor reported that two servants, Tom and Overton, who had well supplied themselves with arms, "joined in the company charges."

During the summer months of 1863, Lt. Col. Arthur Fremantle of the British Coldstream Guards served with the Army of Northern Virginia at Gettysburg. During the retreat through Maryland, he noticed a black Southerner "dressed in full Yankee uniform with a rifle at full cock, leading along a barefooted white man with whom he had evidently changed clothes." When asked to explain, the black Rebel replied: "The two soldiers in charge of this here Yank have got drunk, so fear he should escape I have took care of him." Colonel Fremantle revealed that the black guard spoke to the prisoner "with supreme contempt," adding:

> From what I have seen of the Southern Negroes, I am of the opinion that the Confederates could, if they chose, convert a great number into soldiers. . . . I think that they would prove more efficient than black troops under any other circumstances.

Fremantle also witnessed firsthand the "language of detestation and contempt with which the numerous Negroes with the southern armies speak of their liberators."[51]

Some black Rebels who were captured in battle returned to their masters at the first opportunity, while others readily admitted their loyalty to the Confederacy. Some of the best examples are as follows. Nathan, a servant of the First Georgia Regulars, was captured near Richmond and taken into Union lines. Several days later he returned to Confederate lines with two horses taken from the Union Camp. When Confederate forces retired from Williamsburg, Virginia, a black member of the Twenty-first Mississippi Regiment was left behind owing to sickness. As soon as he had recovered, he slipped through Union lines to join his master. Maj. Henry E. Payton's childhood servant, John, remained away from camp for several days and returned with a pack mule loaded down with booty taken from a Union camp. An Alabama servant who had been in the employ of a Union major was "the first to give us notice that the enemy had

---

[51]Walter Lord, ed., *The Fremantle Diary* (1954).

moved from their front." The black man had left the enemy to return to Confederate forces.[52]

Servants who could have had their freedom often chose to share the hardships of a Northern prison with those whom they had served in the Rebel ranks. Among the troops taken by Union forces at Hatteras in 1862 were two North Carolina blacks who were offered by the Union commander their release in Boston. They politely announced, "We is seches niggers ourselves, sah! We rader stick to our massah, sah."[53]

Bell Wiley found servants "who surrendered with their masters at Vicksburg and who could have had their freedom, [but they] chose rather to share the confinements of prison. Titus, a black South Carolinian, refused to joint his Gettysburg captors and "fight 'ginst my government."[54] Col. W. S. Christian of the Fifty-first Virginia Infantry, who had been captured on the return from Gettysburg and imprisoned on Johnston's Island, reminisced after the war:

> My recollection is that there were thirteen Negroes who spent that dreadful winter of 1863-64 with us at Johnston's Island and not one of them deserted or accepted freedom though it was urged upon their time and again.

Colonel Christian also recalled how one prisoner, George, responded to the prison commander: "Sah, what you want me to do is desert. I ain't no deserter and down South, where we live, deserters always disgrace their families. I'se got a family doen home, sah, and if I do what you tell me, I will be a deserter and disgrace my family, and I am never going to do that."

Capt. Robert Park of the Twelfth Alabama Regiment was imprisoned in Baltimore, where he found Charles, a Georgia servant, who refused to take the oath. Further, to Captain Park's surprise,

> I received a letter from Abe Goodgame, a mulatto slave belonging to Colonel Goodgame of my regiment, who was captured in the Valley and is now a prisoner confined at Fort McHenry, having positively refused

---

[52]*Wadesboro* (N.C.) *Argus,* July 31, 1862; *Charleston Courier,* quoted in *Asheville News,* July 3, 1862; *Richmond Dispatch* quoted in the *Asheville News,* Aug. 21, 1862; *Asheville News,* May 29, 1862; Peter Wilson Hairston Papers, North Carolina Department of Archives and History, Raleigh.

[53]*Asheville News,* June 29, 1862; *Charlotte Daily Bulletin,* July 25, 1862.

[54]*Charlotte Daily Bulletin,* Nov. 10, 1863.

to take the oath. He asks me to write his master when I am exchanged and tell him of his whereabouts, and that he is faithful to him.

In some cases servants continued an attachment to former masters, even though they had run away, were free, or had joined the Union army. The March 21, 1864, issue of the *Fayetteville Observer* carried a story of a Union black soldier who refused to fire into a Confederate regiment on account of "my young master is thar; and I played with him all my life and he has saved me from getting a many whipping I would have got, and I can't shoot thar, for I loves my young master still." Col. Henry Kyd Douglas, formerly of Stonewall Jackson's staff, was wounded and captured at Gettysburg. Imprisoned on Johnston's Island, he was surprised to receive a letter from Enoch, who offered him money and assistance during his captivity. Before the outbreak of hostilities, Enoch had been given his freedom by the Douglas family and was living in Pennsylvania.[55]

To the Confederate army goes the distinction of having the first black to minister to white troops. A Tennessee regiment had sought diligently for a chaplain, but had been unsuccessful until Uncle Lewis, who accompanied the regiment, was asked to conduct a religious service. Soldiers were so pleased that they asked Lewis to serve as their chaplain, which he did from the time of Pittsburgh Landing to war's end. "He is heard with respectful attention and for earnestness, zeal, and sincerity can be surpassed by none," commented the correspondent for the *Religious Herald*. To the men of the regiment as well as to the editors of the Richmond newspaper, the service of the black chaplain was a matter of great pride.[56]

The history of the War Between the States is well documented with accounts of faithful and devoted servants who refused to leave on the battlefield their dead masters' bodies or those who conveyed the body home for burial. John Bakeless noted several cases where loyal slaves, who were pro-Confederate or devoted to their masters (or both), who either spied or willingly offered information to Confederate authorities or withheld information from the Union. Although loyal body servants have been recognized as a distinctive group of black Confederates, the larger contribution to the southern war effort came from thousands of anonymous black Southerners, both slave and free, who tilled the fields, harvested the food, cared for

---

[55] Austerman, "Virginia's Black Confederates."

[56] *Religious Herald*, Sept. 10, 1863.

the plantation and white family, nursed the Confederate wounded in hospitals, and performed a myriad of tasks during the long, four years of war.

Tragically for the Confederacy, the black Southerner was not allowed until the final days of the war to enlist in the Confederate armed forces. The willingness of leaders such as Robert E. Lee, Jefferson Davis, and Pat Cleburne and others to urge emancipation and national service for blacks, when measured against survival as an independent Confederate nation, is telling evidence that slavery was expendable. Had Confederate civil officials fully taken advantage of the southern blacks to fight as allies for their homes and freedom, independence surely would have been gained for the Confederacy. Evidence indicates that as late as March 1865 blacks would have enlisted--and some did enlist--in the Confederate army.

On March 13, 1865, the Confederate Congress reluctantly approved a bill authorizing the President to call upon owners to supply the services of able-bodied men to perform military service. There is evidence that some black soldiers thus authorized by the Confederate government went into battle. A surgeon with the Fourth North Carolina Infantry, writing to his wife from near Petersburg, on March 21, 1865, indicated that "a number of Negroes have already volunteered and are now doing duty as soldiers below Richmond."[57] Among the facts of Winder Hospital Records brought to light, according to James H. Brewer, "perhaps none was more surprising than the evidence that a company of Negro soldiers from Winder and Jackson Hospitals was actually engaged in combat during the defense of Richmond in March, 1865."[58] Winder and Jackson Hospitals were two of dozens of hospitals and hospital facilities in Richmond. Robert W. Waitt, Jr., found Winder and Jackson troops under the command of an individual named Scott, who in March 1865:

---

[57]Shaffner Papers, North Carolina Department of Archives and History, Raleigh.

[58]Brewer, *The Confederate Negro: Virginia's Craftsmen and Military Laborers* (1969).

GEN. PATRICK CLEBURNE WANTED TO UTILIZE SLAVES AS CONFEDERATE SOLDIERS.

> ordered my battalion from the 1st, 2nd, 3rd and 4th divisions of Jackson Hospital to the front on Saturday night . . . . My men acted with the utmost promptness and good will. I had the pleasure in turning over to Dr. Major Chambliss a portion of my Negro company to be attached to his command. Allow me to state, Sir, that they behaved in an extraordinary suitable manner.

Writing to Gen. Richard S. Ewell in the last days of the war, F. W. Hancock indicated that he had

> caused the hired male slaves at this hospital to be convened and after asking them the deliberate question, if they would be willing to take up arms to protect their own from an attacking foe, sixty out of 72 responded that they would go to the trenches and fight the enemy to the bitter end.

Black Confederates were at Appomattox to lay down arms with their white comrades. Pvt. John P. Leach, Company C, Fifty-third North Carolina Regiment, later recalled that his command "stacked arms in front of the victorious Federals on the 10th of April with one lieutenant, nine white men . . . and two Negro servants.[59] In

[59]Georgia Hicks Papers, North Carolina Department of Archives and History, Raleigh.

November 1865, when the Confederate raider *Shenandoah* lowered her flag at Liverpool, a black crew member, Edward Weeks, was also there.

H. T. King found "two free Negroes... from the Belvoir section [Pitt County, N. C.] believed to have served in the army as regular soldiers.[60] They represented numbers of "men of color" who served but whose records are unknown. It cannot be questioned that black Southerners participated in the Confederate war effort at all levels to a greater extent than in the Union effort. Contributions made by southern blacks indicate that they did identify with the Confederacy with loyalty and fidelity both before and after peace was restored.

In the postwar years blacks were honored by white veterans for their contributions to the southern cause. Veteran reunions and parades, monuments and memorials, pensions and eligibility for admission to Confederate soldiers' homes, all testified to the bravery and sacrifice of black Southerners who wore gray. Certainly one old black Confederate spoke for all of his comrades who had fought for Dixie when he uttered in September 1912: "I am proud of my war record." Today, more than a century after the war, that record has been neglected for too long.

---

[60]Blackerby, *Blacks in Blue and Gray.*

CONFEDERATE TROOPS NEAR CHARLESTON, S.C.
Courtesy Library of Congress

SELECTED CORRESPONDENCE

One of the most intriguing sources which documents the wartime experience of black Confederates is personal correspondence. The following letters represent the kind of evidence that is available for researchers. For space and convenience considerations, only those portions of letters which contain references to or were written by black Confederates have been transcribed and printed below.

John N. T. Hammonds (Camp Brown, Knoxville, Tenn.) to "Dear Uncle," Feb. 10, 1862[1]

I seat myself to write you a few lines to inform you that I am well hoping that those few lines may find you all well. I have nothing of importance to write to you at this time. My company is know [*sic*] station on Cumberland Mountain.[2] All but a few of us that was detailed to stay here to mind the tents & take care of some sick boys that we had sick here with the measels. We will all leave here in the morning. We had a small chunk of a fight with the Lincolnit[es] the 2 day of this instant. We killed six of them & taken one prisoner & wouned ten more. Jack Thomas a colored person that belongs to our company killed one of them. . . .[3]

---

[1]Courtesy Special Collections Library, The University of Tennessee, Knoxville.

[2]Hammonds served in the 1st East Tennessee Calvary Regiment, later designated as 5th (McKenzie's) Tenn. Cav., C.S.A.

[3]The military record of one "Jackson Thomas," Pvt., Co. E, 5th (McKenzie's) Tenn. Cav., indicates that Thomas, age 30, was mustered in at Cleveland, Tenn., on Nov. 13, 1861. The record also shows that he was captured at Big Creek on Mar. 14, 1862 and killed on May 14, 1863. Confederate Compiled Service Record, 5th Tenn. Cav., Record Group 109, National Archives.

Lt. L. B. Mitchell (West Point, Ga.) to Bob Williams (Rienzi, Miss.), July 1862[4]

It pains me much to record to you the death of your beloved son Zeb.[5] He deposed this life on Sunday nite at half after two in the morning. His illiness was short after he was taken bad. I will start him home as soon as I can get him ready. John has been a faithful servant to Zeb.[6] I put confidence in him in getting Zeb home. . . .[7]

Wallace Burn (Fort Johnson, S.C.) to "My Dear Master,"[8] Aug. 25 1863[9]

I and Frank have been working in Fort Sumter for 7 days. We returned here on Sunday, where we worked before we went to Sumter. When we were over there, both Frank and I were hurt with bricks, flying from the walls when struck with bombshells. Frank was struck dead for a while but is now recovered. We are both pretty well but are anxious to leave here. It is a very dangerous place on account of shells and cannon balls, and we do not get enough to eat, though worked very hard. Tell all the servants howdy for both of us, and that we are very anxious to see them all again. Please send for us soon as you can. Do write and let us know, when you will send. If you direct your letter to Dr Saml. D. Sanders 21st Regt S.C.V. Charleston S.C. he will get it and read it to us. Good bye master. . . .

---

[4]Contributed by Mrs. Marian Minniece, Houston, Tex. Mitchell was, evidently, Zeb Williams's company commander.

[5]Zeb Williams died at Columbus, Ga., about forty miles south from the town of West Point.

[6]John was a slave belonging to Bob Williams of Rienzi.

[7]It took John nearly eight days to make the 400-mile journey from Columbus to Rienzi. Finally arriving at the old homeplace he had left with his master's son, he was greeted with great rejoicing and many tears among the Williams family.

[8]Rev. James Wilson Burn, who had three sons who fought for the Confederacy, including Henry Cassels Burn, whose papers are a part of the South Caroliniana Collection at the University of South Carolina, Columbia.

[9]Contributed by Bess R. Hubbard of Fuquay-Varina, N.C., the great-great granddaughter of the Reverend Burn.

"Richard" (Greensville, Pitt County, N.C.) to Mrs. Thomas G. Pollock (Warrenton, Va.), Mar. 30, 1864[10]

I received your very kind letter of the 24th of last month yesterday and it made me feel very happy to hear from you and through you from all my friends and acquaintances, and to learn that you were all well. You ask me to tell you all I know of my late dear Master. I am very sorry that I cannot tell you all that you would like to learn. The last I saw of him was just before the battle commenced at Gettysburg and he told me to take off his overcoat from his horse and to take care of it. He then left me and I saw him no more. I was informed that he had been wounded by a shell and wounded in three places, in the head, arm and breast. He fell from the mare he was riding and we were forced to leave him on the field. I would have gone back if I could, but I could not and even if I had gone, I could not have done any good as his spirit had fled and his soul gone up to Him who gave it. I need not tell you my dear young mistress how I felt. I loved him so much having been with him so long. I could not for a long time bring myself to believe that he was gone, but at last the reality burst forth, and I felt lonesome indeed. You ask if he left any relics, any clothes. I am very happy to be able to inform you that his trunk is just as he left it with his new uniform in. It is at Major Traylor's--near Hanover Junction where it was left for safe keeping. I have his bed clothes with me which I use myself. I have his horse and mare in my charge, and I take good care of them. His saddle was robbed on the field of battle. The mare was wounded in one of the forelegs, and she could hardly get back to Virginia but is now nearly well. She got very thin but seems to be picking up now. The horse is in fine trim. After the battle, I staid with Lieutenant K. Nelson until September when I came to Col Joseph Mayo of the 3rd Regiment, and I am still with him. I like him very much, and he is very kind to me indeed. I forgot to tell you that the horse was shot over the right eye, but it did not impair the sight. Please thank your ma for having put herself to the trouble of getting clothes for me. I shall not forget her kindness. I hope she will be happy. I hope that you will not cease to write. I have been expecting a letter from you for a long time. Please let me hear from you all once in a while. I spent 3 days last Christmas with my Mother, and she sends her love to you all. I saw two sisters of mine nearly grown; one named Virginia and the other Martha. I have a fine place now. We live in town. Colonel Mayo has command of this

---

[10]Contributed by Lewis Leigh, Jr., of Fairfax, Va.

post. I am as well satisfied as I can be anywheres away from home. We are not far from the Yankees. We expect to have a fight soon. We had a skirmish last Saturday with some of them. They killed one of our officers and wounded one man. We had 60 men and they had nearly one hundred, but they did not stay long. They ran off just as we got ready to meet them. If you are so kind as to write to me please address your letter to the care of Col. Jos. Mayo, 3rd Reg't Virginia Infty Kempers Brigade Pickets Division Greenville, N.C. . . .

Isaac Calhoun[11] (Camp McDowell, Va.) to "Young Miss" Calhoun (Newnan, Ga.), *ca.* Aug. 18, 1864[12]

After my best Respects I drop you a few lines, and would of done so before now, but I lost your Letter while we was on the retreat. You must give my respects to all Misses Kate & Eugene and also Aunt Lucy & Mary. I wish to know of Uncle Willace Berry how my Little Girl is getting on. I am not well this morning but think I will be well in a day or two as I feel better this morning than I have in a day or too.

I wish you would drop a few Lines to Marter & Let him know that we have lost all of our clothing & so on.

Remember me to Uncle Kato & tell him to give my respects to all of my inquiring Friends in Neunan.

Tell Brother Simmon that I send him a book, witch I think will be of a great deal of importance to him, let me know how his family is all getting on tell him to please write me word.

If my health still improves I shall want to remain in the Army, but if it does not I shall return home soon. Tell Brother to remember me in his Prares. I hope you will excuse a short letter this time for the coach leavs in a few moments.

It is by the Providence of God that we are saved, not by the good general ship of our officers, so with my best respecs I say good bye hoping you will write again soon.

---

[11] Identified as "Capt of Cooking Department," who accompanied his master, Col. J. D. Calhoun, a member of the Newnan (Ga.) Guards.

[12] Printed in the *Southern* (Atlanta) *Confederacy*, on this date.

"Aabram" (Petersburg, Va.) to "Dear Master," Feb. 18, 1865[13]

Desiring much to hear from home, I am having a few lines written to State that I am well and doing well. I am driving a wagon in a Georgia Battalion of Artillery and have been principally engaged during the winter in hauling wood. I am very well satisfied--have a good and a Comfortable house to stay in. I get rations just as the soldiers and draw the same they do.

Give all at home my best love and tell them I am very anxious to hear from there. Tell them I dream about them frequently. I dream of Sarah oftener than of any other. Offer my kindest wishes & feelings to Mistress and accept the same for yourself. Please write to me and give me all the news at home. Let me know if Massa John has been home since I left.

I desire my Mother to receive the money for my corn crop.

Again let me offer my best love to all. Am hoping to hear from you soon. I remain your Obt Servant,

Aabram

P.S. Edmund is here with me driving a wagon also. He desires his best love sent to his wife & children. He says he is in excellent health and much better satisfied than he expected to be. He was fearful when coming that he would have a hard time but is agreeably disappointed.

He says if his Father and Mother are willing, they can draw the money for his corn and keep it until he sees them.

He sends his best respects to "Niely Jane Holb" and say "Howdie" to all his fellow servants.

If you will be so kind as to write to me, address me in care of Maj. John Lane, Sumter Arty Battn 3rd Corps.

Aabram

---

[13]Contributed by Lewis Leigh, Jr., of Fairfax, Va.

STEVE EBERHARDT, CONFEDERATE VETERAN
Courtesy Georgia Department of Archives and History

A regular at Confederate reunions, Everhardt appeared in the video "Echoes of the Blue and Gray." In a 1921 Rome, Georgia, newspaper, he was referred to as "the ancient Senegambian who dresses up in flags and feathers, mostly before Confederate reunion time." Eberhardt gained renown during the war for his prowess in securing food for Confederate soldiers.

★ THE BLACK CONFEDERATES ★

WAYNE R. AUSTERMAN

LATE IN APRIL 1862 GEN. GEORGE B. MCCLELLAN'S MASSIVE ARMY of the Potomac was besieging the old Virginia city of Yorktown, while Gen. John B. Magruder's Confederate troops were holding the Yankees at bay before their fortifications. As the cautious McClellan dugin for a hard fight, he called up his heavy guns to oppose what were in many cases only painted logs frowning back at him from the embrasures of Magruder's fieldworks. For as long as the Confederates could deceive and delay McClellan, they were buying precious time for the defenders of Richmond to prepare the city's defenses and to muster a counterblow against the bluecoats' ultimate drive westward along the marshy peninsula that rose between the York and James rivers.

For a considerable time during the siege at Yorktown, Union troops in the forward trenches were plagued by a phenomenally-accurate Rebel sharpshooter. Working under the direction of an officer and firing from the cover of a bunker or ruined house, he continually sniped at the invaders. The marksman became such a nuisance that members of the elite 1st U.S. Sharpshooters were ordered to take concealed positions and to try to eliminate him. One night, after carefully studying for several days their opponent's firing positions, the green-uniformed infantrymen sent a patrol out to take cover close to the southern lines. The next morning they spotted the Rebel taking his position and killed him with a single volley.

McClellan's soldiers had found the sniping worrisome enough, but even more disturbing was the disclosure that the slain enemy marksman had been a Negro. Tales of the deadly "darky sharpshooter" spread throughout the Union camp, and the daring black's exploits were subsequently recorded in the postwar regimental history of the 1st U.S. Sharpshooters. To men who had been raised on the fulminations of William Lloyd Garrison and *Uncle Tom's Cabin*, it seemed incomprehensible that any black man could willingly serve the Confederacy.

Wayne Austerman received his PhD from Louisiana State University in 1981.

Although the Yorktown marksman might have been dismissed as a lone eccentric, the fact is that black Southerners, both slave and "free men of color," made important contributions to the Confederacy's struggle for independence. While every black in the South naturally craved personal freedom, many of them also shared a distinctively-southern attachment to their native soil. Moreover, they dreaded the South's despoliation by any invader, even one who promised "emancipation." Although the passage of a Union force nearly always triggered a joyful exodus of slaves from the fields, there were also those who realized that a future raked from the ashes of their homeland was a poor prospect for any man, slave or free.

When the war began in April 1861, approximately 5.5 million whites and 3.5 million blacks lived in the South, with all but 130,000 of the blacks being slaves. As the conflict intensified and continued, both the labor of blacks and their loyalty became increasingly vital to the Confederacy. The postwar stereotype of the "faithful darkies" is grossly exaggerated. While the war did bring increasing unrest among the plantation slave populations, and many slaves did use the pressures of the war to test concessions from their owners, there were no mass uprisings as had been dreaded by antebellum whites. For most of the war slave conduct is best characterized by what might be termed "hopeful acquiescence." Blacks realized that if the North won they would be free, but if the South won there was still hope for grateful white recognition of their loyalty. Therefore, slave and free blacks labored in the fields and factories for the dream of southern independence, while some even bore arms in defense of the homeland they shared with their masters.

To perceptive southern blacks, the new Confederate government did not represent "a society closed in defense of evil institutions," as one prominent historian has put it, but rather a potential arbiter of change for the better. Although the Confederate Constitution guaranteed the preservation of slavery as a social and economic institution, it also explicitly banned resumption of the foreign slave trade and made no punitive references to the status of existing free blacks. The leaders of the new government were essentially moderates, not the radical fireeaters who dreamed of extending slavery throughout North America. The new republic's president, Jefferson Davis, was noted for the liberality with which his family operated their plantation, where slaves served as their own managers and magistrates. With such men providing leadership, one could hope that a grateful and prosperous South might be generous in victory to all of her people.

"Black labor was vital to the Confederacy and the black impact upon southern life as, if anything, greater in wartime than in peacetime," one scholar has asserted. "Yet the converse was true as well. The Confederate experience had a profound effect upon black life in the South---so much so that by mid-1863 the southern black experience had undergone subtle but profound metamorphoses." Even had the South won her independence, relations between the races would have been irrevocably altered by the shared experience of struggle. The war had made the skills and labor of every black person doubly important, and the demand for such skills had brought many blacks into relative prominence.

When Johnny Reb went to war, he carried a rifle that may well have been assembled by black artisans in one of a score of arsenals, both public and privately operated. His uniform was spun from fibers plucked by black hands and his haversack carried food planted and harvested by black laborers. Without slaves who tended crops, cared for livestock, and staffed forges, tens of thousands of white men would have been forced to remain at home to keep the southern economy functioning, thereby robbing the field armies of precious strength in an already uneven contest with a numerically-superior enemy.

Blacks also joined Confederate soldiers in camp and on the battlefield to perform a myriad of important tasks. Black gang labor erected massive earthworks which protected southern cities and seaports from attack. Black teamsters drove teams which pulled the Confederate army's supply wagons, and black men comprised many of the crews which kept the Confederacy's pitifully small but vitally important railroad network in operation. Although the Confederate government eventually resorted to impressing slaves from their owners in an effort to provide needed manpower for military construction projects, many blacks served willingly in every job that was open to them.

The spirit of black voluntarism, like that of the whites, burned most fiercely in the early months of the war. In April 1861 a company of freedmen in Nashville, Tennessee, volunteered for state service at the governor's discretion, and in Memphis the authorities opened a recruiting office for blacks eager to wield a shovel or to drive a team for "The Cause." In June 1861 the Tennessee legislature authorized Gov. Isham Harris to enlist for service "all male persons of color between the ages of fifteen and fifty." Three months later a body of several hundred black sappers (engineers) and their white officers marched proudly through town. The *Memphis Avalanche* remarked that "they were brimful of patriotism, shouting for Jeff Davis and singing war songs." In Lynchburg, Virginia, the local paper applauded the enlistment of seventy free blacks in the state forces, saying "three cheers for the patriotic Negroes of Lynchburg."

The willing labor of such men was an incalculably valuable asset to the southern war effort. Whether they served as body servants or as government workers, blacks were a common sight in every Confederate army camp. Few Confederate veterans could not later recall with gratitude and affection a black servant who helped with the camp fatigues or cooked their meals. Some of them became legendary figures in the army.

The Confederate soldier was by necessity a resourceful creature, but his ingenuity paled before that of the regimental cooks. One such individual was dubbed "General Boeyguard," in honor of his masterful culinary stratagems. During Lee's invasion of Pennsylvania, "Boeyguard" left the line of march at dawn and did not return until the troops had halted for the night, when he would appear happily laden with hams, fowls and other produce appropriated from local farmers. Another cook, Bill Doins, a freed black who acquired his nickname from his habit of calling his cooking utensils "my doins," had spent the prewar years on a Chesapeake Bay oyster boat. But when Virginia seceded he immediately joined the colors. After the battle of Sharpsburg in September 1862, Lee's battered army was retiring southward after fighting a much larger Federal force to a bloody standstill near the tiny Maryland town. In the confusion of the movement, Bill became separated from his "doins." The men had to eat, and there was flour at hand in the supply wagons. Therefore, Doins fashioned an impromptu bakery on the shores of the Potomac, mixing flour with river water right in the barrels and using rails from a nearby fence as fuel for the baking fires. As each company in his regiment reached the fording place, they found hot loaves of bread ready to be thrust on their ramrods as they passed by the tireless cook's *al fresco* kitchen. Probably the most famous cook in the army, Jeff Shields, served the staff officers' mess of Gen. Thomas J. "Stonewall" Jackson. Shields made certain that the often-preoccupied general and his harried staff were properly fed before starting one of their famous marches. After the war Shields was a fixture at veterans' reunions, proudly appearing in full Confederate uniform, with his coat bedecked with medals, ribbons and badges.

Young Southerners went off to war with body servants in tow, and military life tended to create strong bonds between them. As Bell Wiley observed in *Embattled Confederates*: "Close association and exposure to common hardships tended to promote cordial and affectionate relations between soldier masters and their colored attendants. In battle some of the servants proved their fidelity and courage by risking their lives to seek out wounded masters and remove them to places of safety." There were many such instances of devoted comradeship, and neither party involved ever seemed to feel that they were incongruous.

One of the most notable such friendships occurred in the 43rd North Carolina Infantry. Lt. George W. Wills marched off to war with his manservant, Wash. On September 19, 1864, Wills died in battle at Fisher's Hill, and the literate, obviously intelligent, slave wrote a grieving letter to the dead soldier's brother, saying: "I am willing to do anything I can do to help out our struggling country. I desire to see you and talk with you. . . . Master Richard I know something about trouble." Wash was joined by other slaves who felt similar ties of home and family to their masters. The leading diarist of the war, Mary Boykin Chestnut, related the story of a Columbia, South Carolina, black who braved bursting shells on the battlefield to carry a bucket of ham and rice to his owner. The *Linden Jeffersonian* of August 8, 1862, told the story of a Virginia slave who was involuntarily liberated by a Union officer. "The Negro was sent to a spring to procure some water for his new master," reported the journal, "but instead of performing that task he kept on his way to the Confederate lines, where on his arrival he presented himself to (the commanding general) together with two horses which he captured from the Yankees on his 'masterly retreat!' "

Inevitably, camp slaves soon came to view their masters' fight as their own, and they begin to take an active role in the struggle. Capt. George Baylor of the 12th Virginia Cavalry recorded how one of his servants "rendered himself obnoxious to the Yankees by luring a detachment of blue coats into a Rebel ambush." In June 1863, during the great cavalry battle at Brandy Station, Virginia, two of Baylor's servants, Tom and Overton, seized discarded enemy weapons and joined the regiment as it charged. Capturing a black servant of some Federal officer, they marched him back to camp at gun point and held him prisoner for several months. The two warriors were happy to have had their own menial laborer to relieve them of the burden of their chores.

Such incidents became increasingly common as servants seized muskets and joined their white comrades on the skirmish line. Capt. Arthur L. Fremantle of Her Majesty's Coldstream Guards, who toured the Confederacy in 1863 and was present at Gettysburg, told of seeing "a most laughable spectacle" during the march back to Virginia. "A Negro dressed in full Yankee uniform, with rifle at full cock, leading along a barefooted white man, with whom he had evidently changed clothes. General [James] Longstreet stopped the pair and asked the black man what it meant." The proud warden explained that the two soldiers who had originally taken charge of the prisoner drank too deeply of the brandy in their canteens and, fearing the Yank's escape, turned him over to their servant. Fremantle was struck by the slave's "consequential manner" and "the supreme contempt with which he spoke to his prisoner." The Englishman found that reality gave the lie to much Northern propaganda. "This little episode of a Southern slave leading a white Yankee soldier through a Northern village, *alone and of his own accord,* would not have been gratifying to an abolitionist," Fremantle observed. "Nor would the sympathizers both in England and in the North feel encouraged if they could hear the language of detestation and contempt with which the numerous Negroes with the Southern armies speak of their liberators."

The black auxiliaries were undoubtedly disconcerting to the invaders. The 8th Texas Cavalry ("Terry's Texas Rangers") rode through the western theater of the war accompanied by as many as 500 slave servants. They repeatedly proved their worth to the graycoats. In the fall of 1864 part of the regiment shadowed Sherman's army as it rampaged through Georgia, ambushing stragglers and meting out .44-caliber justice to the looters it captured. One company was sleeping soundly in camp just before dawn when a slave warned them of an approaching Union patrol. The Texans quickly faded into the woods and then pursued the Northerners to strike them by surprise.

LT. COL. ARTHUR FREMANTLE OF THE BRITISH COLDSTREAM GUARDS.
Courtesy National Archives

The Federals captured by the Texans often were in for a rude surprise. One cavalry officer related how he was held under guard by a shotgun-wielding black who kept the weapon trained on the Yankee's head with unwavering concentration. "Here I had come South and was fighting to free this man," the disgusted major wrote in his diary. "If I had made one false move on my horse, he would have shot my head off."

The inhabitants of Indiana and Ohio must have been equally mystified in the summer of 1863, when Gen. John Hunt Morgan led his Kentucky and Tennessee cavalrymen on a thousand-mile sweep through the Ohio River Valley, spreading panic and confusion as they went. Northern farmers and townsmen were astonished to see scores of blacks accompanying the raiders. A doggerel ballad of the day went: "Morgan, Morgan, the raider, and Morgan's terrible men/ with Bowie knives and pistols are galloping up the glen." The poet might have given a stanza to the slaves who rode in their stirrups with carbines ready.

The blacks and Morgan's men shared close bonds. Before the war Kentucky hosted a relatively mild form of slavery, and many bluegrass blacks enjoyed a *de facto* state of emancipation the moment they mustered with Morgan's companies. Morgan returned their loyalty after one of his troopers was found guilty of stealing a freedman's shirt. The general had him publicly punished. "Old Box," Morgan's personal servant, was a fanatical Confederate. During the Ohio raid large numbers of Union militiamen were overpowered and forced to march along in the dust beside their captors. "Box" delighted in mocking the bluecoats with the question: "Don't you want to ride?" Morgan finally made him quit taunting the miserable prisoners.

Eventually, the Union forces rallied and mounted a determined pursuit of the Rebels. Their line of retreat blocked, Morgan's raiders were brought to bay near the Ohio-Virginia border and badly beaten in a battle. Morgan and over a thousand troopers sought to escape by swimming their mounts across the Ohio River. Raked by musketry from the shore and the cannon of a Union gunboat, many of them never survived the crossing. Morgan urged "Box" to stay behind in the safety of Union territory. Ignoring the bullets which whined past them, Box replied indignantly: "Marse John, if they catches you, they may parole you, but if this boy is catched in a free state he ain't going to git away while the war lasts."

As the Union armies marched deeper into the South, they encountered increasing numbers of black combatants. During the Vicksburg Campaign, Grant's troops met them in battle on several occasions. A correspondent for the *New York Times* wrote: "The guns of the Rebel battery were manned almost wholly by Negroes, a single white man, or perhaps two, directing operations." At the Battle of Chickasaw Bayou, reporter Thomas Knox of the *New York Herald* came under fire from an unexpected source. "On our right a Negro sharpshooter has been observed whose exploits are deserving of notice," he told his disbelieving readers. "He mounts a breastwork regardless of all danger, and getting sight of a Federal soldier, draws up his musket at arm's length and fires, never failing of hitting his mark. . . . It is certain that Negroes are fighting here, though probably only as sharpshooters."

Perplexed and angry, the Union troops could not fathom why southern blacks should voluntarily serve their oppressors. Tens of thousands of slaves had already flocked to Union camps throughout the South in search of freedom. So, why did these deluded bondsmen fight for the slaveowners? The more candid among them might have admitted to themselves that, while slavery was widely despised among the Federals, few of them had great liking for the slaves as people. Racial prejudice was deeply ingrained in most whites, North or South, and the slaves they freed often suffered at their hands. In *The Life of Billy Yank,* Bell Wiley noted: "One who reads letters and diaries of Union soldiers encounters an enormous amount of antipathy toward Negroes. Expressions of unfriendliness range from blunt statements bespeaking intense hatred to belittling remarks concerning dress and demeanor."

There were attitudes prevalent in many northern units that could have pleased the most rabid modern klansman. "I think that the best way to settle the question of what to do with the darkies would be to shoot them," remarked a New York soldier to his family. In early 1863 a young Bostonian stationed in occupied New Orleans confessed: "As I was going along this afternoon a little black baby that could just walk got under my feet and it looked so much like a big worm that I wanted to step on it and crush it, the nasty, greasy little vermin was the best that could be said of it."

Such feelings were often expressed in violence. At Paducah, Kentucky, fugitive slaves were stoned by a midwestern regiment when they tried to enter Union lines. In South Carolina a mob of soldiers from the 47th New York Infantry gang-raped a seven-year-old Negro girl. The men of an Illinois regiment watched and cheered as a comrade molested a slave woman. Pvt. Elisha Stockwell of the 14th Wisconsin Infantry recalled a Union officer serving in the occupation force at Montgomery, Alabama, who was fired with reforming zeal and determined to see the freedmen educated, whether they liked it or not. The captain convened a school for the local black children and rigidly enforced their attendance. When one boy bridled at being taught the alphabet, he received punishment in the best Puritan tradition by being staked out face up in the blazing sun, while the captain "sat on the porch in the shade and tantalized him, and gloated over his way of punishment."

Understandably, quite a few blacks preferred their old, familiar relationships with southern whites to the possible terrors of acquiring a new set of masters. Emancipation opened the door to a very uncertain new world, as the freedmen of Nashville, Tennessee, learned to their shock in the winter of 1864, when Union troops conscripted them at bayonet-point for service in the work gangs building fortifications against Hood's Army of Tennessee.

Inevitably, the question of enlisting black troops for combat service arose. From the outset of the war, blacks served as military bandsmen. A photograph survives from 1861 showing black musicians mustering under the colors with their white comrades of Company K, 4th Georgia Infantry (Sumter Light Guards), and numerous other contemporary illustrations attest to the widespread acceptance of black fifers and drummers. Josephus Black and two other servants of Gen. John B. Gordon braved Union musketry to give Gordon's troops a tune as they marched into battle. The Confederate Congress passed legislation requiring that black and white military bandsmen receive the same pay. Martial airs and country ballads played by blacks cheered many a homesick Rebel around the campfire at night or put extra swing in his step as he joined the skirmish line.

It was not a large step from tapping a drum to drawing a ramrod. There was no apparent lack of willing recruits for the sable regiments. A visitor to Charleston, South Carolina, in 1861 observed "the thousand Negroes who, so far from inclining to insurrections, were grinning from ear to ear at the prospect of shooting the Yankees." In June 1861 the Tennessee legislature authorized the governor to accept for military service all male persons of color between the ages of 15 and 50. By that time one Negro company from Nashville already had joined a white regiment in marching east to fight in Virginia. By February 1862 state legislators were actively considering a law to organize all free blacks for possible military service.

Although President Davis and many other officials were hostile to the idea of arming blacks to defend the Confederacy, as the war continued and the casualty lists grew agonizingly longer resistance began to moderate. By the war's midpoint the Union government began forming black combat units, which proved beyond any doubt that with good leadership the former slaves and free blacks could fight well.

Meanwhile, the Confederate States Navy had never hesitated to enlist black sailors. The C.S.S. *Chicora,* an ironclad gunboat based in Charleston Harbor, counted three free blacks among its company. On January 31, 1863, the *Chicora,* accompanied by another ironclad, the C.S.S. *Palmetto State,* steamed out to confront a Union flotilla. The *Chicora*'s guns set one Yankee steamer ablaze, damaged two others, and then turned their fury on the U.S.S. *Keystone State,* a large side-wheeled steamer. The Union shells bounced harmlessly from the gunboat's armor, while the *Chicora*'s cannon sent round after round, ripping into the steamer's fragile wooden hull. Only the Union ship's superior speed allowed her to escape certain sinking by the feisty Rebel vessel's guns.

Photographic evidence from the period reveals that black tars also served on the most famous vessel in the Confederate Navy, the C.S.S. *Alabama.* Commanded by Capt. Raphael Semmes, this sleek cruiser terrorized Yankee merchant men from Long Island Sound to Capetown. A photograph taken of two of his officers lounging against one of *Alabama*'s guns shows a black seaman standing in the background.

In November 1864, President Davis still opposed black enlistments "until our white population shall prove insufficient for the armies we require." The men shivering in the trenches around Petersburg might have told him that such a time had already come and gone. That same month Secretary of War James A. Seddon refused permission to an officer in Columbus, Georgia, to recruit a regiment of black riflemen. Even in the face of official resistance, the idea would not disappear. Before his death at the battle of Franklin on November 30, 1864, Gen. Patrick R. Cleburne of the Army of Tennessee advocated the use of black troops. Other senior officers in the army endorsed the proposal. Judah P. Benjamin, Davis's Secretary of State, urged the emancipation of those slaves who would fight for the South, arguing that, if such men were willing to stand by their masters to defend the homeland, they fully deserved their own freedom.

By February 1865 Davis finally had abandoned his objections to arming the slaves, concluding "that all arguments as to the positive advantage or disadvantage of employing them are beside the question, which is simply one of relative advantage between having their fighting element in our ranks or in those of the enemy." A month earlier Gen. Robert E. Lee had recommended black enlistments in a letter to Senator Andrew Hunter, maintaining: "I think we must decided whether slavery shall be extinguished by our enemies and the slaves be used against us, or use them ourselves at the risk of the effects which may be produced upon our social institutions. My own opinion," Lee continued

> is that we should employ them without delay. I believe that with proper regulations they may be made efficient soldiers. . . . Our chief aim should be to secure their fidelity. . . . Such an interest we can give our Negroes by giving immediate freedom to all who enlist, and freedom at the end of the war to the families of those who discharge their duties faithfully (whether they survive or not), together with the privilege of residing at the South. To this might be added a bounty for faithful service.

Had Lee, Benjamin, and Davis had their way, slavery would have been ended as an act of policy to secure southern independence. Those who continue to insist that the South fought the war simply to defend slavery should ponder their words in the twilight hour of the Confederacy.

Ironically, at least one free man of color was regularly enlisted in a Confederate unit. John Wilson Buckner, nephew of a prosperous South Carolina black who held numerous supply contracts with the Confederate forces, joined the 1st South Carolina Artillery on March 12, 1863. He served gallantly until wounded in action at Battery Wagner in Charleston's defenses on July 12, 1863. "Although everybody knew Buckner was a Negro, personal associations and a sterling family reputation nullified the law and made Buckner an honorary white man as a soldier," so wrote his family's chroniclers.

Despite the support of prominent leaders such as Lee and Cleburne, the Confederate Congress waited until March 13, 1865, to enact legislation authorizing the enrollment of slaves in the Confederate Army. According to the measure, each state was required to furnish 300,000 men for duty. A handful of black units were actually organized, and at least one uniformed company was seen drilling in the streets of Richmond only a few weeks before Appomattox. None of these companies ever burned powder in their nation's defense, but that fact did not diminish the worth of the contributions previously made by so many others.

Freedom came to southern blacks at last, but it was the liberty of the pauper. Whites and blacks alike suffered well into the next century from the wanton destruction inflicted on their land by the invaders, who claimed to have been fighting in defense of high moral principles. Reconstruction and the crude attempt at social engineering that accompanied it drove a wedge between the races, inspiring far deeper bitterness and mistrust than ever had existed during the war. The appearance of hooded nightriders and the passage of Jim Crow laws were two of the results.

Even during the grimmest days of Yankee occupation, white and black Southerners recalled with pride the times when the gray ranks had swept forward to meet the enemy, marching in tune to the battle hymn played by black musicians:

We are a band of brothers
And native to the soil
Fighting for our liberties
With treasure, blood and toil

CLEBURNE'S MEN HOLDS SHERMAN'S FORCES AT MISSIONARY RIDGE, NOV. 25, 1863.

CONFEDERATE MILITARY RECORDS

Although most southern blacks were never officially mustered into Confederate service, many do appear in extant military records. The following selections have been excerpted from the compiled service records of black Confederates in the National Archives, Record Group 109, as well as from original muster rolls located in the Georgia Department of Archives and History, Atlanta, and in the North Carolina Department of Archives and History, Raleigh.

MUSTER ROLLS OF GEORGIA INFANTRY REGIMENTS

Name	Regiment	Military Occupation
Aaron	3rd Battn.	musician
Abraham	63rd Ga.	cook
Benger, Charles	2nd Battn.	musician
Black, Solomon	13th Battn.	musician
Brice, George	Read's Indpt. Co.	musician
Burroughs, Luke	63rd Ga.	chief cook
Burroughs, Lydia	63rd Ga.	cook
Burroughs, Sam	13th Battn.	cook
Davidson, William	1st Ga. (Olmstead's)	drummer
Davis, Bacchus	Read's Indpt. Co.	musician
Dawson, Catharine	63rd Ga.	cook
Dawson, Hannah	63rd Ga.	cook
DeLyon, Charles H.	1st Ga. (Olmstead's)	musician
Fox, Joe	63rd Ga.	nurse
Greene, Charles	26th Ga.	musician
Griffin, Lucius	54th Ga.	musician
Harris, Alexander	1st Ga. (Olmstead's)	musician
Harris, Peter	2nd Battn.	musician
Harvey, Simeon T.	1st Ga.	musician
Jones, Nelson	63rd Ga.	nurse
McCleskey, Henry	1st Ga.	musician
Middleton, Maurice	1st Ga.	musician
Miller, Joseph	1st Ga. (Olmstead's)	
Morgan, Eliza	63rd Ga.	nurse
Morgan, Ellen	63rd Ga.	nurse
Morris, Ellen	63rd Ga.	nurse
Ranger, Abram	63rd Ga.	asst. cook
Riley, David	30th Ga.	musician

MUSTER ROLLS OF GEORGIA INFANTRY REGIMENTS (cont.)

Name	Regiment	Military Occupation
Savally, Henry	26thGa.	musician
Schley, Wesley	2nd Battn.	musician
Waters, William	1st Ga. (Olmstead's)	musician
Whittle, John	2nd Battn.	musician
Yopp, Bill	14th Ga.	drummer
Young, William	1st Ga. (Olmstead's)	drummer

COMPILED SERVICE RECORDS OF VIRGINIA REGIMENTS

Name	Regiment	Military Occupation
Adams, Lewis	Richmond Howitzers	cook
Alex	7th Va. Cav.	teamster
Allison, William	Howitzers	
Anderson, John	1st Co. Howitzers	
Armisted	7th Va. Cav.	teamster
Ben	7th Va. Cav.	teamster
Bob	3rd Co. Howitzers	cook/teamster
Bob	Va. State Rangers	servant
Brown	7th Va. Cav.	teamster
Brown, Thornton	Charlottesville Art.	servant
Burwell, Carter	32nd Va. Inf.	chief cook
Carrell, Oscar	32nd Va. Inf.	chief cook
Carter, Richard	1st Co. Howitzers	cook
Chapman	Charlottesville Art.	servant
Charles	Goucester Co. Guards	cook
Chisman, Oliver	32nd Va. Inf.	cook
Cyrus	7th Va. Cav.	teamster
Drew, Edmund	Charlottesville Art.	barber
Ephraim	1st Co. Howitzers	cook
Ezekiel	32nd Va. Inf.	cook
Gaines, Lucian	7th Va. Cav.	teamster
George	32nd Va. Inf.	cook
Grant, Thornton	7th Va. Cav.	servant
Gustin	32nd Va. Inf.	
Harrison, William	1st Co. Howitzers	servant
Henry	7th Va. Cav.	teamster
Hiram	7th Va. Cav.	teamster
Horace	7th Va. Cav.	teamster
Humbles,James	1st Va. Cav.	bugler
Jackson, George	7th Va. Cav.	servant

COMPILED SERVICE RECORDS OF VIRGINIA REGIMENTS (cont.)

Name	Regiment	Military Occupation
Jackson, Robert	61st Va. Inf.	cook
Jim	7th Va. Cav.	teamster
Jim	Charlottesville Art.	servant
John	7th Va. Cav.	teamster
John, "Black Hawk"	7th Va. Cav.	cook
Jones, William	32nd Va. Inf.	cook
Kean, Aleck,	2nd Co. Howitzers	cook
Lewis	7th Va. Cav.	teamster
Mayo, Henry	56th Va. Inf.	
Mayo, Joe		servant
Nelson, W. B.	32nd Va. Inf.	cook
Oliver	7th Va. Cav.	driver
Page, Charles	32nd Va. Inf.	cook
Sergerant, Horace	1st Co. Howitzers	driver
Smith, Charles	32nd Va. Inf.	cook
Smith, G. W.	32nd Va. Inf.	cook
Strother	7th Va. Cav.	teamster
Tatem, Samuel	61st Va. Inf.	
Taylor	7th Va. Cav.	driver
Texas	32nd Va. Inf.	cook
Thomas	32nd Va. Inf.	cook
Tom	2nd Co. Howitzers	servant
Tom	7th Va. Cav.	servant boy
Tom	7th Va. Cav.	teamster
Walker, Chilse	32nd Va. Inf.	chief cook
West, Richard	32nd Va. Inf.	cook
Williams, Edgar	1st Co. Howitzers	cook
Woodford, Edward	4th Va. Cav.	servant/cook
Yerby, Joe	9th Va. Cav.	cook

BLACK CONFEDERATES OF NORTH CAROLINA

Name	Regiment	Military Occupation
Anderson, Sam	6th N.C. Inf.	body servant
Bynum, Brinkley	15th N.C. Inf.	
Dempsey, Charles	36th N.C. Inf.	captured at Ft. Fisher
Dempsey, Henry	36th N.C. Inf.	captured at Ft. Fisher
Dove, Willis	63rd N.C. Inf.	cook
Doyle, J.	40th N.C. Inf.	captured at Ft. Fisher
Dunston, Tom	8th N.C. Inf	cook
Evans, Jackson	3rd N.C. Inf.	
Fletcher, Sandy	23rd N.C. Inf.	
Griffin, Sam	24th N.C. Inf.	body servant
Hayes, Everett	10th N.C. Inf.	private
Herring, Daniel	36th N.C. Inf.	captured at Ft. Fisher
Howard, Elisha	15th N.C. Inf.	
Hunter, Frank	23rd N.C. Inf.	
Liggins, Will	13th N.C. Inf.	
Lynch, Will	63rd N.C. Inf.	cook

BLACK CONFEDERATES OF NORTH CAROLINA (cont.)

Name	Regiment	Military Occupation
Newcom,James	1st N.C. Btn.	private
Poisson, James	10th N.C. Btn	musician
Powell, Amos	23rd N.C. Inf.	body servant
Reed, Arthur	40th N.C. Inf.	private
Reed, Miles	40th N.C. Inf.	private
Revels, Henson	1st N.C. Btn. Hvy. Art.	private
Revels, William C.	21st N.C. Inf.	fifer
Rudd, William	63rd N.C.	cook
Sykes, Caleb	10th N.C. Btn. Hvy. Art.	musician
Venable, John W.	21st N.C. Inf.	
Ward, Lawrence	10th N.C. Inf.	cook

MONROE GOOCH.

Born in the year 1844, in Davidson County, Tennessee. Entered the Confederate Army as cook with Capt. Wm. Sykes of the 45th Tennessee Infantry, and remained with him and Capt. Henry Irby, and true to the cause until the close of the war, and is now proud to be numbered with the Veterans of 1861-1865. He had permission to visit his home at the time of Hood's raid into Tennessee, and could have remained, but true to his principles, he returned to Capt. Sykes, and remained until the surrender.

MONROE GOOCH, CONFEDERATE VETERAN
Courtesy Tennessee State Library and Archives

A 1902 pamphlet entitled "Biographical Sketches and Stories of Company B, Confederate Veterans of Nashville, Tennessee" includes this photograph of Monroe Gooch, who served with the 45th Tennessee Infantry, C.S.A

[APRIL 12, 1862.—For Pettus to Beauregard, reporting number of men at the various rendezvous in Mississippi, preparing to enter the Confederate service, see Series I, Vol. LII, Part II, p. 301.]

AN ACT for the payment of musicians in the Army not regularly enlisted.

The Congress of the Confederate States of America do enact, That whenever colored persons are employed as musicians in any regiment or company, they shall be entitled to the same pay now allowed by law to musicians regularly enlisted: *Provided,* That no such persons shall be so employed except by the consent of the commanding officer of the brigade to which said regiments or companies may belong.

Approved April 15, 1862.

GENERAL ORDERS, No. 23.

WAR DEPARTMENT,
ADJT. AND INSP. GENERAL'S OFFICE,
Richmond, April 15, 1862.

Parties who have been authorized by the War Department to raise troops in Texas are prohibited from enlisting or receiving twelve-months' men, and all authority heretofore granted by this Government to raisè troops in any State is hereby revoked, unless the organization is completed and the muster-rolls returned to this office within sixty days from the date of this order.

By command of the Secretary of War:

S. COOPER,
Adjutant and Inspector General.

EQUAL PAY FOR BLACK MUSICIANS IN CONFEDERATE SERVICE: AN 1862 ACT.

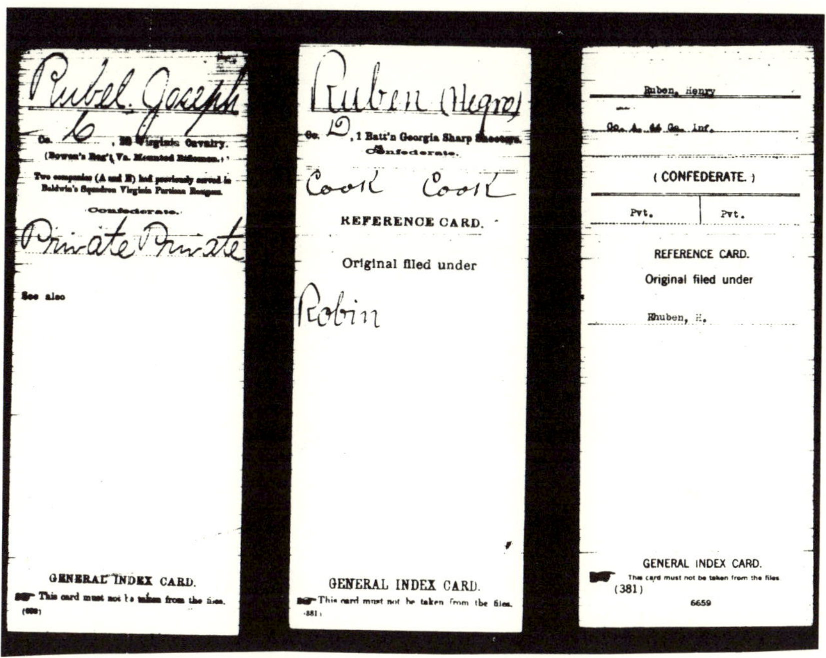

Rubel, Joseph
Co. C, 22 Virginia Cavalry.
(Bowen's Reg't, Va. Mounted Riflemen.)
Two companies (A and B) had previously served in Baldwin's Squadron Virginia Partisan Rangers.
Confederate.
Private Private
See also
GENERAL INDEX CARD.
This card must not be taken from the files.

Ruben (Negro)
Co. D, 1 Batt'n Georgia Sharp Shooters.
Confederate.
Cook Cook
REFERENCE CARD.
Original filed under
Robin
GENERAL INDEX CARD.
This card must not be taken from the files.

Ruben, Henry
Co. A, 46 Ga. Inf.
(CONFEDERATE.)
Pvt. Pvt.
REFERENCE CARD.
Original filed under
Rhuben, H.
GENERAL INDEX CARD.
This card must not be taken from the files
(381)
6659

EXAMPLES OF COMPILED SERVICE RECORDS FOR CONFEDERATE SOLDIERS LOCATED IN THE NATIONAL ARCHIVES. THE CENTER CARD IDENTIFIES A NEGRO SERVING WITH A GEORGIA UNIT. NOTE THAT HIS MILITARY OCCUPATION IS LISTED INSTEAD OF HIS RANK.

673

Stewart, Wiley

Co. H, 4 (Murray's) Tennessee Cavalry.

(Confederate.)

CARD NUMBERS.

1 4828 4449

Number of medical cards herein 0

Number of personal papers herein 0

Book Mark:

See also

S | 4 Cav. (Murray's) | Tenn.

Confederate.

Wiley Stewart

Capt. Q. C. Sanders' Company, Tennessee Cavalry.*

Age ...... years.

Appears on

Company Muster-in Roll

of the organization named above. Roll dated

Camp Myers, Oct 1, 1861.

Muster-in to date July 22, 1861.

Joined for duty and enrolled:

When Aug 24, 1861.

Where Camp Zollicoffer

By whom J. H. McHenry

Period 12 months

Valuation in dollars of horse

Remarks: Free person of color

*This company subsequently became Company H, 4th (Murray's) Regiment Tennessee Cavalry.

Companies B and F, 5th Battalion Tennessee Cavalry, which were not transferred with the other companies of that battalion to the 2d (Ashby's) Regiment Tennessee Cavalry May 24, 1862, formed the nucleus of an organization that appears to have been known as Spiller's Battalion Tennessee Cavalry. This battalion was increased to a regiment about August, 1862, by the addition of other companies and was known as the 4th Regiment Tennessee Cavalry, Companies B and F, 5th Battalion Tennessee Cavalry becoming Companies I and C, respectively, of this regiment. The regiment appears to have been disbanded about January [illegible], [illegible], and Companies C, F, H and I becoming B, I, C and H, respectively, of the 8th (also called 4th) Regiment Tennessee Cavalry; Companies A and D became Companies D and C, respectively, 1st Regiment Confederate Cavalry, and Companies B, E, G and K became Companies H, K, G and F, respectively, 22d Battalion Tennessee Infantry.

Book mark:

J. W. Wilkinson
Copyist.

COMPLIED SERVICE RECORD OF WILEY STEWART, 4TH TENNESSEE CAVALRY, A "FREE PERSON OF COLOR."

Alexander (Negro)

Co. B, 24 Texas Cavalry.

Wilkes' Reg't.
2 Texas Lancers.
2 Reg't Carter's Brig.

Became Co. I, Granbury's Consol'd Texas Brig., about April 9, '65.

(Confederate.)

CARD NUMBERS.

1	45488559	20	
2		21	
3		22	
4		23	
5		24	
6		25	
7		26	
8		27	
9		28	
10		29	
11		30	
12		31	
13		32	
14		33	
15		34	
16		35	
17		36	
18		37	
19		38	

Number of medical cards herein —

Number of personal papers herein —

BOOK MARK:

See also

(Confederate.)

A 24 Cav. Texas

Alexander

Co. B 24 Texas Cavy.

Appears on a

Roll of Prisoners of War

received at Camp Butler, Ill., Jan. 31, 1863.

Roll dated not dated, 186 .

Where captured

When captured , 186 .

Remarks: Negro Liberated

Roll bears the following indorsement: "Received City Point, Va., April [illegible] 1863, from Jno. E. Mulford, Capt. 3d Infty. N. Y. V., Comdg. 'Flag of Truce,' (on the within rolls) Eight Hundred & Eighty three (883) Confederate Prisoners of War paroled for Exchange; also Two Surgeons.

J. H. THOMPSON, *Capt. Comdg. Post.*"

Number of roll: 12

(639b)

E. E. Rawson, *Copyist.*

COMPILED SERVICE RECORD OF A CONFEDERATE PRISONER OF WAR "LIBERATED" FROM CAMP BUTLER, ILLINOIS.

EX-CONFEDERATES BUCHANAN, W. L. DRAKE, & UNCLE LEWIS NELSON (*ca.* 1920).
Courtesy Tennessee Historical Quarterly

★ A TRIBUTE TO LOYAL CONFEDERATES ★

JAMES L. HARRISON

CONFEDERATE MEMORIAL DAY WAS DESIGNED TO PAY HOMAGE to those who at great sacrifice devoted their lives and fortunes to a just cause of defending their homeland and to the principle of states' rights. Sometimes we have failed to reflect on the diversity of the men to whom we pay tribute and to all who deserve our special honor on this day. For example, significant support was given to the Confederacy by Native Americans, including the Choctaw, Chickasaw, Cherokee, and Creek. Another source of support often overlooked came from Hispanic Americans, particularly the forces led by Col. Santos Benavides of Laredo, Texas, who kept the Confederate flag flying over the state capitol at Austin throughout the war. Yet there is another sector of contribution to the Confederate war effort often overlooked but who faithfully upheld the southern cause: African Americans. The support given by black Southerners to the Confederacy has become the most hidden fact of history in the annals of our Republic. Indeed, black Confederates are casualties of history, lying in unmarked graves all over the South.

Black Confederates were part and parcel of the economic war machinery which sustained southern armies. The Confederacy could not have withstood four years of Federal onslaught without black labor in various areas of production and service, as well as in the construction of fortifications. Many slaves accompanied their masters or other family members to war and provided loyal service under circumstances where they could have run away. Many others served in military support roles, such as cooks, teamsters, and laborers. As a slave from Bexar County, Texas, remarked: "If every . . . black had thrown 'way his hoe and took up a gun to fight for his freedom along with the Yankees, the war'd been over before it began."

Numerous blacks also saw military action under the Stars and Bars. Many served without benefit of uniform or of official governmental sanction, at least until late in the war. Lacking such things did not prevent blacks throughout the South from volunteering their services to the Confederacy. For example, in April 1861 a company of blacks in

---

Adapted from the June 1992 edition of "Dispatch," a membership newsletter of the Confederate Historical Institute, Little Rock, Ark.

Nashville, Tennessee, offered themselves to military authorities. The following month a recruiting effort was organized among free blacks in Memphis. On June 28, 1861, not long after Tennessee had officially withdrawn from the Union, the state legislature authorized the governor "at his discretion, to receive into the military service of the state all male free persons of color between the ages of 15 and 50." While there were no black regiments formed, a number of individuals served in various regiments in the South throughout the war. Slaves fought side-by-side with their masters at First Manassas in August 1861, and a "number of Africans," who were said to have been in a ravine from which heavy fire had been directed at the Federal army, were captured by Sherman's forces at Griswoldville, Georgia, in July 1864.

After the war white Southerners remembered their former slaves' loyalty by erecting monuments, some of which still stand. At Fort Mill, South Carolina, for example, a monument's inscription reads, in part: "Dedicated to the faithful slaves who, loyal to a sacred trust, toiled for the support of the army with matchless devotion, and with sterling fidelity guarded our defenseless homes, women, and children during the struggle for the principles of our Confederate States of America." There is a similar monument at Canton, Mississippi, and in 1907 the Tennessee Division of the United Confederate Veterans adopted a resolution recognizing the faithful conduct of slaves during the war.

Let it never again be said that the war was fought to free the slaves. Let us on this Confederate Memorial Day pay tribute to all who faithfully supported the Cause, particularly black Southerners who also fought to defend their homeland from the Yankee invaders.

MEMORIALS, MARKERS, & TRIBUTES

Testimony to black loyalty to the Confederacy can be seen across the South in cemetery headstones, historical markers, stone monuments, and larger obelisks, as shown in the examples reproduced below.

VIEWS OF THE MONUMENT TO A FAITHFUL SERVANT, CANTON, MISSISSIPPI
Courtesy James West Thompson

AN UNKNOWN CONFEDERATE HOSPITAL ATTENDANT'S GRAVE IS MARKED BY A VETERAN'S HEADSTONE, ALONG WITH THOSE OF HIS FORMER COMRADES, IN THIS SMALL CEMETERY NEAR MADISON, GA. *Courtesy Emory Lavender*

John Davis, carriage driver for the Jefferson Davis family, holds a flag at the spot where President Davis, his family, and a small force of cavalry camped on the night of May 8, 1865, two days before his capture in Irwin County, Ga. The marker depicted in this photograph is four miles from Eastman and was erected in 1918. *From History of Dodge County*

"AND TO YOU OUR COLORED FRIENDS . . . , WE SAY WELCOME. WE CAN NEVER FORGET YOUR FAITHFULNESS IN THE DARKEST HOURS OF OUR LIVES. WE TENDER TO YOU OUR HEARTY RESPECT AND LOVE, FOR YOU NEVER FALTERED IN DUTY NOR BETRAYED OUR TRUST."

Col. William Sanford
From an address given before a reunion of the 7th Tenn. Cav., at Columbia,Tenn., on Sept. 22, 1876.

SLAVES AND FREE BLACKS SERVING AS TEAMSTERS.
Courtesy Arthur Shilstone & Smithsonian Magazine

VIEW OF THE MONUMENT TO FAITHFUL SLAVES, FORT MILL, SOUTH CAROLINA
Courtesy The Confederate States of American-Historical Preservation Society

OFFICERS ELECTED

UNITED CONFEDERATE VETERANS

Commander-in-Chief — GENERAL WILLIAM B. HALDEMAN, Louisville.

Adjutant General—GENERAL A. B. BOOTH, New Orleans.

DEPARTMENT COMMANDERS

Army of Northern Virginia—GENERAL CHARLES B. HOWRY, Washington.

Army of Tennessee—GENERAL JAMES A. THOMAS, Dublin, Tenn.

Trans-Mississippi Department—GENERAL E. W. KIRKPATRICK, McKinney, Tex.

Next Meeting Place—Memphis.

SONS OF CONFEDERATE VETERANS

Commander-in-Chief — W. MC DONALD LEE, Richmond, (re-elected).

Historian—ARTHUR JENNINGS, Washington, (re-elected).

Executive Council—JUDGE EDGAR SCURRY, Texas, (re-elected).

DEPARTMENT COMMANDERS.

Army of Northern Virginia—DR. W. C. GALLOWAY, North Carolina.

Army of Tennessee—RALSTON F. GREEN, New Orleans.

Trans-Mississippi Department—JAMES S. DAVENPORT, Oklahoma.

GILBERT SUTTON in *The Item*

"ALL THE HEROES WEREN'T WHITE"
From "The Stars and Bars" (1923)

DR. JAMES B. AVERITT, ONE OF THE FIRST CHAPLAINS IN THE ARMY OF NORTHERN VIRGINIA, AND "BLACK HAWK."

JEFFERSON SHIELDS, STONEWALL JACKSON'S COOK (ca. 1908).

★ AGED BODY SERVANTS AMONG THE LAST ★ SURVIVORS OF THE CONFEDERATE ARMY

JAY S. HOAR

JUST AS BODY SERVANTS BECAME A DISCERNIBLE ELEMENT, CADRE, OR component, who served from the earliest weeks of the war throughout most units of the Confederate army, so, too, would they surface eighty or more years later as a distinct identity among our far-dwindled last grand old Boys in Gray. Given the reality of their strong survival in the 1940s and after, we may readily appreciate several truths: 1) that their original numbers within the Confederate fighting machine during 1861-65 was likely up into the 30,000-range or more; 2) that, percentage-wise, they more than "held their own" as post-centenarian Gray at near-mid-20th century; and 3) that their preeminently outdoor, physical, low-stress lifestyles contributed to their impressive capacity for survival.

Perhaps it would be well to recapitulate or to summarize points made earlier in this study as to which segment of southern society they came from and what their precise roles were within the Confederate military at large. They were primarily able-bodied house servants of the more comfortable whites, rather than fieldhands; they were male blacks who had shown a willingness and adeptness for literacy and gentle manners, who had often won the hearts of their owner-employers and enjoyed positions of trust and privilege. Often they were treated as family, and this relationship had been true for generations. For the overwhelming crisis which ensued that dread first April of an eventual five, they had their own nommes-de-guerre: "Old Time Unpleasantness," "The Reb People's War," "The Reb Time," "The Ce-Sesh War."

What more natural in the spring of '61 than for many of these trusted servants to accompany a family's son(s) upon departure to do patriotic duty in the C. S. A.? It was a matter of pride for them to do so. Their valued services effectually augmented the manpower of the southern armies. While some soldiers had more than one body servant, this number was exceptional. Most, of course, had none. Often one body servant served from three to as many as eight soldiers, each

---

Jay S. Hoar is Professor of American Studies at the University of Maine, Farmington.

of whom contributed toward the servant's support.[1] Many servants were obligated chiefly to one soldier. Soldiers from non-slaveholding families sometimes hired blacks to be their body servants, though some did engage in actual fighting with the foe (a truth that endured as gratifyingly solid).[2] Body servants of all ages--14 up through 60, perhaps--were indispensable for handling the brunt of a variety of vital chores. Salient among these tasks were cooking, washing, foraging, cleaning, hostelring, digging for all purposes (trenches, graves, redoubts, latrines), and, when in jeopardy, protecting the lives of their white companions. Not a few gave their lives by shielding their soldier from a fatal blow, though most of them were commonly kept back from the battlefront itself. Some performed sad chores of ushering their soldier's body home. While the North bolstered its already larger military ranks with some 187,000 black troops in segregated regiments, the South adhered, remarkably, to its valiant code of honor by restricting its blacks to paramilitary duties, even to the closing weeks of the conflict.

Our errand today is to attempt to identify some of the most aged body servants of the Confederate army, yet living seventy-five years after and later. Realistically, it is hardly possible to account for all of their last remnant who survived some eighty postbellum years. But, because celebrity status slowly winded its way to their door, we may, after some twenty-three years of investigating, present a comprehensive tabulation. As we get into the mid-to-late 1940s, this accounting still falls short of definitive. The proud record they laid down for posterity speaks eloquently in this roster of standouts among our centenarian Gray:

---

[1]Bell I. Wiley, "What Manner of Men," *The Life of Johnny Reb*, 327.

[2]Ibid, 328. "But a few [body servants] became so thoroughly imbued with the martial spirit as to grab up muskets during battle and take pot shots at the enemy. There are several instances on record of servants thus engaged, killing and capturing Federals. On at least one occasion Confederate domestics made prisoners of Negroes serving Yankee officers. When fighting abated, the colored aide usually loaded himself with canteens and haversacks and went in search of his master. If the latter was wounded, the servant carried him to shelter and sought medical assistance; if he was killed, the domestic made arrangements for his burial or escorted the body home."

NAME	HOMETOWN	DEATH	AGE
Jeff Mabry	Hopkins County, Tex.	1929	110
Albert Everett[3]	Murfreesboro, Tenn.	1933	105
Steve Eberhardt	Rome, Ga.	1935	105
Ransom Simmons	Taylor, S.C.	1937	105
Parson R. Williams	Stansbury, Md.	1938?	113
James Lucas	Natchez, Miss.	1938	104
Nick Carter	Arcola, Miss.	1938?	111
Wm. H. Singleton#	New Haven, Conn.	1938	103
Joseph C. Richeson	Rockbridge Cty., Va.	1941	94
E. Burrell Scruggs	Huntsville, Ala.	1941	95?
Turner Hall, II*	Hugo, Okla.	1942	99
Simon Phillips*	Birmingham, Ala.	1942	96?
Willis Branch	Prince Edward Cty., Va.	1942	96
Butler Calvert	Northampton Cty., N.C.	1943	98
Peyton Coles	Prince Edward Cty, Va.	1943	95
Mark Thrash* #	Chattanooga, Tenn.	1943	120
Arthur A. Reese#	Waukesha, Wis.	1943	103
James Mayberry	Centreville, Tenn.	1945	95
Washington Ratliff	Anson Cty., N.C.	1945	100
James McKinney	Richmond, Va.	1945	100
Pompey Tucker*	McKenney, Va.	1946	99
Frank McGhee*	Oxford, N. C.	1946	110
Robert Wilson*	Elgin, Ill.	1948	112
Geo. St. Pierre Brooks#	Winnipeg, Can.	1948	103
Lewis Carter*	Lanexa, Va.	1949	99
Simon Douglas#	Fairview, N. J.	1950	107
Alfred T. Blackburn*	Hamptonville, N.C.	1951	109
Hattie Carter[4]	Greensburg, Pa.	1956	121+

*=Biographical profile follows #=Served later in Federal forces

What little I have learned of the lives of these noble human kind I gladly share. Would that my inquiries have begun forty years sooner than they did, our knowledge of the last among them had been ampler.

One of the most colorful personalities was "Uncle Steve" Eberhardt of Rome, Georgia. "He declared his mistress sent him to war to look out for her son. . . . 'My principal job was to get all the chickens used in the army. I don't recall failing to deliver them.' " Proverbial at his prowess at raiding roosts, Eberhardt after the war attended all U.C.V. reunions within reach and invariably was decorated with

---

[3]Virginius Dabney, *The Last Review: The Confederate Reunion*, 34 (photo), 38, 39.

[4]Hattie Carter gets an honorable mention here, for she carried for several months food and ammunition to the Confederate soldiers about Richmond, Virginia, and likely saved a number of lives.

chicken feathers and well plastered with reunion ribbons.[5] In her August 27, 1984, note from Rome, Mrs. F. W. Ray recalled: "I saw 'Uncle Steve' on Broad Street, Richmond, waving the Confederate flag as he gathered money to go to reunions. He served a Capt. Eberhardt through the war. He worked later at the Marshall Mfg. Co. of Rome, Georgia."

When Jeff Mabry died on June 7, 1929, he was reputed to have been 110 years old. Recognized as the only black man from Hopkins County, Texas, to have served with the Confederate army, "Uncle Jeff" was 101 years old on March 26, 1920, when he married Sarah Jeter. According to the 1920 Federal census for Hopkins County, Mabry was 101 years old at the time and a native of Georgia. When Hinche Parham Mabry, an attorney in Jefferson, Texas, answered the call to colors on June 13, 1861, "Uncle Jeff" joined him, and both were assigned to Company G, 3rd Texas Cavalry. They served the entire war with their unit until it surrendered in May 1865. Uncle Jeff took great delight in being known as the "Head Chicken Thief of the 3rd Texas Cavalry." After the war Jeff Mabry returned to Hopkins County, where later in life he was well cared for by former Confederate soldiers, provided with a place to live, food to eat, and medical attention when needed. He attended the monthly meetings of the Mat Ashcroft Camp #170, U.C.V., in Sulphur Springs, Texas, and all of the Confederate reunions up until the year before his death. He died while ex-Confederates were meeting at Charlotte, North Carolina, in 1929.[6]

Turner Hall, II, born October 11, 1842, in North Carolina, often told stories of his servant days in the war. He seldom failed to speak of his having been an orderly for Gen. Robert E. Lee (possibly so, but unverified). He was brought to Hugo Oklahoma, by Judge Trice from Mississippi, about 1906. Hall went to the Diamond Battle Reunion at Gettysburg in 1938 and later appeared on "We, the People" radio show in New York City. Widely respected by all who knew him, he was buried (according to Otis E. Hays, Jr., of Pierce City, Mo.) near Nettleton, Mississippi.[7]

---

[5] Dabney, *Last Review*, 39.

[6] Research on Jeff Mabry provided by Wilbur Thomas Myers of Sulphur Springs, Tex

[7] Jay S. Hoar, *The South's Last Boys in Gray*, 18.

"Uncle Simon" Phillips, of Norwood, on Birmingham's north side, served many years as president of Alabama's Ex-Slave Association. Originally he had been a slave on a Hale County plantation. He traveled widely, signing up former slaves and Confederate war veterans to join; his aim being to get them a state pension. In 1930, for example, he found 375 ex-slaves and recorded their age, name of former master, and any honors they received during the war. By 1935, Phillips had missed but two of forty-six Confederate reunions. In 1930 the association had two thousand members. At the 1931 reunion, Matt Gray of Huntsville told a news reporter, "I was an eye-witness to Gen. Lee's Surrender." Gray had first gone to the war as a body servant to a soldier who had died. He later accompanied Capt. John Lewis when they saw "Stonewall" Jackson, lifeless, days after Chancellorsville.[8]

For years Gray (who lived from March 18, 1828 to March 25, 1928) worked as a janitor at the Madison County Court House, in Huntsville, where he often met with fellow comrades of Egbert Jones Camp, U.C.V., among whom was Essex Lewis (ca. 1821-1927), a highly respected comrade who died in Birmingham. Born a slave of Col. Nick Lewis of Morgan County, Essex was a body servant to Capt. Cam Patterson in Virginia. "Uncle Essex" was a farmer and later janitor at the Huntsville Post Office. At his request, his funeral was held at the home of his friend, Matt Gray.[9]

Mark Thrash, born December 25, 1822, living beyond the age of Moses, is one of a limited number of those last survivors of the war who fought under both Federal and Rebel flags. These men had first served on the Confederate side, were captured, and then chose manumission by signing up (the famous "X" in some cases) to serve in the Federal army, often in the unit that took them prisoner. One of these ex-Confederates was William Henry Singleton of New Haven, Connecticut, who, having just ridden down the line of march in the 72nd National Encampment Parade of the G.A.R. at Des Moines, died minutes later, "going on in" in glory. Singleton, a native of New Bern, North Carolina, belonged first to "Marse Thomas Singleton," serving in Company K, 2nd North Carolina Infantry. But he eventually ran away and became a servant to Maj. Robert Leggett of the 10th Connecticut. He attained the rank of first sergeant, and he is said to have been the only black officer to have raised, drilled, and trained

---

[8]*The Birmingham News*, Feb. 28, 1978.
[9]Hoar, *Last Boys in Gray*, 12.

a regiment of black troops in the war. He was at the Blue-Gray Gettysburg Reunion in July 1938.[10]

Then there was Arthur Reese, born November 2, 1840, of Waukesha, Wisconsin, who at twenty-one had joined the Confederate army as hostler in a South Carolina cavalry unit. He was eventually captured by a Colonel Putney of a Wisconsin cavalry outfit, and he became an orderly to Putney.[11] George St. Pierre Brooks was born January 1, 1845, on a Brooksville, Kentucky, farm, where at age four he last saw his mother being auctioned off to a wealthy family. "I was mostly a houseboy, though sometimes they'd put me out in the fields," he recalled. When the war came, George followed as personal servant to Captain Scofield, his master's son-in-law, until they were captured near the Ohio River by the 7th Ohio Cavalry early in 1865. Now twenty, during those closing three months of the war, George took care of horses for the Federals. But nine-tenths of his wartime duties had been for the Confederacy.

After the war, while running footraces for P. T. Barnum's Shows (1865-66), George turned in a 9-3/4th-seconds-100-yard dash. He joined the famous Fisk Jubilee Singers and traveled widely, singing Negro spirituals and giving a command performance before Queen Victoria, before leaving the troupe in 1879. Brooks was cook-butler-caretaker for wealthy families in Kentucky, Indiana, Missouri. In 1911 he chose to do farming at Westbourne, Manitoba, with Dr. William Hartford of Champaign, Illinois. In 1917, still tall and statuesque, he approached an army recruiter, honestly stating his age: seventy-five. Initially refusing him, the recruiter retreated: "If you'll sign up as 40, we'll take you." He did, enlisting as a cook in the Canadian Expeditionary Force and serving in France. Between the world wars Brooks cooked in Winnipeg, renewing old friendships with singer Paul Robeson and with Joe Lewis, having known "the Champ" as a lad in Detroit. Twice married, he survived his wives, and his only daughter left with no known relatives. Late in 1944 he began living at Deer Lodge Military Hospital. One fine day in 1946, while visiting veterans, Viscount "Monty" Montgomery hailed Brooks as "a real soldier." Brooks, in turn, hailed Canada "a fine country where I've

---

[10]Hoar, *New England's Last Civil War Veterans,* 10. Singleton's story arises partly from a 1922 account told by Mrs. Laurel F. Vlock and Joel Levitch, co-authors of the 196-page juvenile biography *Contraband of War.*

[11]*Waukesha* (Wis.) *Freeman,* Dec. 28, 1943.

never known unhappiness." Today he is claimed in the military plot of Winnipeg's Brookside Cemetery.[12]

Returning to Mr. Thrash: His parents, natives of Africa, were brought from Jamaica to Virginia, where Mark Thrash was born on Dr. Christopher Thrash's plantation. Mark was man-grown when Doctor Thrash bought acreage from the Indians in Meriwether County, Georgia. "Massah Doctah sent 'bout sixty slaves thar to make a camp an' clear land. Most three years later the doctah moved to ar new plantation. We'd been thar most twenty years when the war broke out. Nowadays [1930s] the younger kinfolk o' the doctah's comes to see me 'bout onct a year, on an average."

A full forty practically by the spring of '61, Mark Thrash eventually became a servant and handyman in both Confederate and Union Armies, with nearly equal time in each. His probable first battle experience came when he was sent by Doctor Thrash to see one of the Thrash boys who had gotten wounded at Chickamauga. He served on burial details, those grave consequences of battles. Thrash saw as much of Chickamauga's horrible after-scenes as any man did. He performed menial duties with the Gray-clads until taken prisoner, concluding the war rendering similar duties for the other side. But no paperwork exists whereby he could be said ever to have joined any unit.

Thrash "refugeed" to Arkansas as a laborer. Perhaps lured by news of the first annual reunion of the U.C.V., he settled in 1890 in Chattanooga, where he worked two years on construction for the Central Georgia Railway. For the next thirty years he was a civil service employee, a groundskeeper and guide at the Chickamauga-Chattanooga National Military Park. At length, he retired in 1922, a few months shy of 100 years. Thrash's government pension was for his park work, not for the time he put in with either Rebs or Yanks. He was closer to the Rebs in his sympathies, though, like the last living participant of the war--Sylvester Mack Magee of Hattiesburg, Mississippi--he tried for a Federal pension but failed to get it for lack of records. In his speaking of various battles, Thrash noticeably pronounced the "ou," as in "fought," as "ow," as in "now" or "cow," a revealing antebellum dialectic touch.

---

[12]*Winnipeg Free Press,* Jan. 5, 1938; May 7, 1948. See also Canadian Dept. of Veterans Affairs News Release, May 22, 1946.

What were his topics? He would tell you Indian stories, of his sitting down to "bow-wow" meat with them, of their campfires and his watching them dance. He would tell you of his personal friend, Gen. Henry V. Boynton, "father of Chickamauga Park," for whom he had been a bodyguard. He would show you his log cabin collection room filled with mementos of U.C.V. reunions and park celebrations. Perhaps his proudest possession was a faded blue colonel's coat given him by Boynton himself. According to Thrash, the coat once had been worn by General Grant, who had given it to Boynton when Grant was promoted to brigadier-general. One may well wonder why "Uncle Mark" went so often to U.C.V. reunions rather than to G.A.R. meets. The Rebs were always good to him, and he proudly wore their badges of 1913, 1921, 1924, and 1934 on his lapels.

Who was to say Uncle Mark was not entitled to attend as many U.C.V. functions as he chose? If ever a veteran could carry off with pure charm the ambivalence of belonging to the Gray and the Blue, that fellow was Uncle Mark Thrash. Certainly one of Tennessee's last grand old Gray and the eldest of its ex-slaves (at the time), he had fathered twenty-nine children by his first three wives. In 1934, his oldest son, living in Los Angeles, was ninety-two, while his youngest was, to the best of his recollection, fifty-six. Only in the 1930s did Uncle Mark truly gain recognition nationally as the oldest voter and pensioner. For these distinctions he appeared on CBS radio programs in 1936, 1940, and again in May 1943, on "We, the People." In June, at nearly 120 years Mark donated his hot water bottle to the scrap rubber drive. That year he still had good vision, adequate hearing, and his own teeth.

We see him as others last saw him--sitting on his log-cabin porch, rocking easy, hair white as newly-driven snow, a cob pipe going, while he marvels at a passing "airship." "No, missus, I wouldn't go up in one of them flyin' machines fo a million dollahs. No, missus, thems too fast fo me. . . . I'm not goin' up thar till I goes to stay." He didn't go to stay until just a week before his 121st birthday. Leaving his fourth wife, Jessie, and eighteen of his children, he was given, appropriately, military honors from Friendship Baptist Church and was buried in District Hill Cemetery near Chickamauga.[13]

---

[13]*Chattanooga News-Free Press*, Sept. 23, 1931; *Chattanooga Times*, Apr. 3, 1934; Dec. 18, 1943; *Chattanooga Post*, Jan. 13, 1969. See also, Norris McWhirter, comp., *Guiness Book of World Records*, 26, which refers to Uncle Mark this way: "The 1900 U. S. Federal Census for Crawfish Springs Militia District of

The last personality among body servants who did duty on both sides in the American Iliad was Simon Douglas --discovered only in May 1985 by the writer via Dr. Richard W. Lenk, of Paramus, N.J.-- born January 25, 1843, on a Fairfield County, South Carolina, plantation. A houseboy who had acquired skill at horseshoe making, Douglas went off in 1862 to the battlefront as a body servant to several family sons. Once his master's sons had died or had gotten killed or their unit captured (mid-1864), Simon chose to win his freedom as a bummer (forager), moving northward with the Blue-clads. In all his senior life, Simon did not play up either his southern or northern duties in the war. In 1866, Simon, age 23, arrived in Fairview, New Jersey, where for seventy years he worked as a blacksmith.

In his January 8, 1987, letter from Fairview, Dominick T. Majetta, age 67, volunteered:

> I remember Mr. Douglas well. On warm days he took sun in his yard. He was nearly blind; his hair, snow white. My father, who died 15 years ago at 93, told me Douglas shod horses for him. In the mid-1940's Louis Battaglia, Mayor of Fairview 1950-64, tried to get a Civil War pension for Douglas, but to no avail. The federal government said his name was not entered on Union Army muster rolls. Everyone in town knew of the effort. As far as I know, he couldn't read or write. He said he shod horses for the cavalry, another reason he was allowed to accompany the federal troops. He never claimed enlistment. Earlier, he dug trenches and tended horses for the South, but wasn't a Confederate, as far as actual soldiering.

In his February 10, 1987, letter from Fairview, Michael Orecchio, 82-plus-years old, parliamentarian, consultant, teacher, lecturer, conveyed these thoughts:

> Since Fairview is only 8/10 ths of a square mile--535 acres, I never lived more than a quarter mile from the Douglas residence. As a five-year-old, I first knew Mr. Douglas in 1909. He was about 5' 10", physically and morally strong. His house was a faded yellow, two stories. His blacksmith shop fronted on Broad Avenue. My father, Anthony, for years had brought his horses for shoeing. During the early 1900's the price for four shoes--ice cleats and hoof pads (where indicated)--was about $2. Douglas claimed to be the first Negro to cast a vote in this part of the world. Until 1900 the yearly taxes on his property were $15. From then on they rose rather sharply. By 1937 Simon owed $2,382 to Fairview. The humanitarian concept of

---

Walker County, Georgia, records an age of 77 for a Mark Thrash. . . . He would have survived for 121 years."

> municipal tax relief for the elderly, currently in vogue, is a relatively recent practice. . . . This family maintained their pride and dignity in the face of crushing financial adversity--lack of employment, sickness, progressive loss of Simon's sight, low income. My immediate concern, at the time, was to stay the eviction of the Douglases from their old homestead and to stand by them in their hour of need. Everyone who participated in the SIMON DOUGLAS FUND demonstrated assurance that there were people in Fairview who cared about their plight. With sensitivity we set up that fund. The *Bergen Evening Record* committed itself to the project that fall of 1949 and we raised the needed funds. We are a little richer because the Douglases lived among us.

Mary Douglas gave her father the best of home care. The eldest of New Jersey's Civil War personalities, Simon lapsed into a coma his final two days. He was laid to rest in the Hackensack Cemetery--grave 4738, Sect. 26, Row 12.[14] He brought to five the number of states whose last veterans of Our Saddest War were blacks: Isaiah Fassett, who died June 24, 1946, at 102, in Wilmington, Delaware; Joseph Clovese, who died July 13, 1951, at 107-plus, in Pontiac, Michigan; Alfred T. Blackburn, who died December 15, 1951, at 109-plus, in Hamptonville, North Carolina; and Sylvester N. Magee, who died October 15, 1971 at 130-plus, at Columbia, Mississippi.

Simon Douglas was a personality whose mettle was crafted in the forge of human life, whose beauty only improved under the hammering of daily living. For him no pensions, no parades, no monument, no flag. In lowliness he came and went and dwelt among us. Given that through the whole armor of his lowliness there shone the choice alloy of a spiritual loftiness, we can only conclude: "Dis chile got wings."

One of the last four surviving body servants was Frank McGhee, whose story is best told as it unfolded (with great effort) for the writer.[15]

It is 7:00 a.m., June 23rd, 1983, a bright, humid day, as the writer strolls a mile north on Highway 96 from the Holiday Inn to downtown Oxford, North Carolina. He has a light breakfast--Southern style biscuit-'n-egg and coffee. With a poplar walkingstick and notebook in

---

[14]Michael Orecchio, comp., *This Town Called Fairview,* 10-11, 54; *Bergen* (Hackensack, N. J.) *Evening Record,* Mar. 9, 1950; *Hudson* (Union City, N. J.) *Dispatch,* Nov. 23, 1939.

[15]McGhee's approximate age is predicated on the fact he was born in the neighborhood north of Oxford, N. C., the same year as Betty Parish, great-aunt of Nat Burwell, who turned 82 in 1983.

hand, he resumes his northerly heading, having the previous evening learned that the McGhees live well out of Oxford itself on rural Route 4. Although he first discovered his subject's identity in an old, heavy ledger at the Office of the State Auditor in Raleigh some forty-nine months earlier, the writer has made but slight gains on learning about "Frank McGhee--112--Body Servant, Deceased 9/16/ 46." Hence, this grassroots effort. A short lift to the outskirts of Oxford with Dr. Sam Daniels proves interesting. "Why, yes, I knew Frank McGhee. Doctored for him a few times. I moved here in 1946. He died a few months after. There are McGhees up on 96. Walk west till you hit 96 then strike north."

By 8:30 a.m. the writer, two miles out, sees a lady hanging out a washing. She is Mrs. Pearl Finch, age ninety. Slowly entering her field of vision so as not to startle her, he greets her. "Did you ever know Frank McGhee, the old Confederate veteran?" "Ah, yes, I did. I moved here in 19 and 38. He lived a mile up the road t'other side. The Huntsville Baptist, you say? Why, yes. It's about almost three miles more on your right, I reckon."

In fifteen minutes the writer sees a mailbox "SULA McGHEE." He is pleased to find it, having the evening before phoned her, the widow of David McGhee (1885-1964), son of Frank. As agreed, she will be home by 1:30 p.m. from town and will be glad to help. The hiker finds the new brick Huntsville Baptist Church, sitting back, a cemetery behind. According to his death certificate (dated October 8, 1946), Frank is buried out here. After three thorough walk-throughs, it is apparent his grave is unmarked (and for all practical purposes, not exactly known--a deep regret). Here's a Leonard H. McGhee (1913-1966) and a Ulysses McGhee (1886-1965). A tiny metal funeral marker is all he ever had to identify his resting place, lost to the wind, to a mower, to time, lost likely some thirty years before.

By 9:30 the sleuth approaches and enters a crossroads grocery-hangout. "Are there any McGhees living nearby?," he asks. The man at the register offers, "A Frank McGhee lives up the road here on 96, a mile, I'd call it, on your left. The place is just out of view." A fellow going north in a pickup gives the outsider a lift. "Say, maybe you should call in at Matt Harris'. See that old place unpainted, with the porch? He's right there now, been there for years--112 years old, they say. He knew your man for sure." Thanking the driver, the

"UNCLE FRANK" MCGHEE AT 105
Author's collection

grateful rider follows a winding dirt road 800 feet into the woods. Young Frank, 64, the namesake, is elated to tell what he knows of his uncle. "He was an older brother to my father, Alec McGhee, who died when I's seven. I don't know much about 'im. Just that he farmed. Lived where Sula lives in the old place. Alec, my brother, could tell you more. He lives over on Route 4 about three miles maybe. Yes, Matt Harris knew 'im."

Walking back a mile, the notetaker arrives at the Harris place. It is 10:09. A grandson answers the knock and soon leads the way off to the right to Matt's front room, where shades are fairly much drawn. There on the foot of his bed he is, half sitting, half prone, propped up by pillows. Smiling and offering his hand to the visitor, Matt's easy testimonials tumble forth natural as sweet potato pie:

> I ain't never harmed nobody. I ain't scared o' the Devil. I been praying since I's ten years old. I's been prayin' 102 years. I's in Methuselah's class. When I born? March 19, 1871, over in Person County, Roxboro way. People was scarce when I's born. But I's had twelve chillum. First thing each mornin' when I wakes, I knows--The Savior have brought me through the night. What you here fo? Frank McGhee?
>
> Some claims he was 116, but he was closer to 105, I b'lieve. Not much mo. Frank wasn't a smart farmer--only grew an acre or two. He raise corn, tobacco, a little burley, a few vegetables. Never sold much. Yea

> suh, he bought the old Huntsville Church fo' his home an' there he live. Married Robert Ragland's daughter, Anne.
>
> I've cut 14,000 miles of right of way under the powerlines to the Virginia border and back 1936-42. My favorite food? Cornbread an' sausage. I enjoys real coffee. Frank? Frank never been in trouble. We met at church--the Huntsville. We'd sit in brush arbor, too. He went to church regular right to the last. We's good neighbors fo years. I's to his funeral. I walks to the sto' an' sometimes to the church, but uses two sticks fo balance. I ain't never helped the Devil. Nor Frank ain't neither.

Matt Harris senses his caller would like to see him walk. The grandson puts on Matt's left sock and shoe (size 11-1/2) and the visitor puts on the right. Matt stands, stooped a bit, but, unaided, without a cane, he walks directly out of the house and across the porch. He sits on a hard chair and suggests his guest try some of the ripe cherries on the tree nearby. They are indeed tasty. Departure is at hand. Matt Harris, 112, so spiritually "at-one-ment" with his world and Maker, whom to know is to be closer to Frank McGhee, lays a deliberate blessing upon his retreating admirer. It is 11:15 a.m.

By noontime, the invader from Farmington, Maine, walks into the farmyard of Alec McGhee, Jr., age 66, who is supervising a harrowing. "We all called him Uncle Frank. His stature was small, almost spindly. We all went to his funeral. No, he never had no stone. He's up front somewhere near the church, I b'lieve. He lived where Sula lives today. Lillian Puryear an' her brother, William McGhee, may know what you're looking for. You came by their house a ways below Sula's towards town. I'll take you there."

Lillian, also age 66, and her brother, 62, are David McGhee's children (as was Leonard, above) by his first wife, Pearl McGhee. They offer that their grandfather wore a mustache, smoked a pipe, chewed a little, walked many times to town, liked any part of a hog including the head, and that when he came to his last, said, "I'm not goin' ter die. I'm just goin' to sleep on away."

Finally, at 12:45, Alec, returning home, leaves off his passenger at Sula's. Sitting up over the highway and perhaps 200 feet back on a wide curve, the old house is a two-story frame structure. Weathered clapboards, unpainted since before the Great Depression, convey a parched dryness of pastel whites, grays and browns unto blacks. Frank and Anne's old dwelling appears much as it did when they last lived in it. The Acme wood and coal pot-belly from the Cameron Stove Co.

FRANK MCGHEE'S LAST HOME, THE OLD HUNTSVILLE BAPTIST CHURCH
Author's collection

in Richmond, Virginia, sits there still, just a few feet from where the old couple warmed themselves.

Annie Ragland McGhee (1846-1952), gravesite today unmarked, was blind the last five of her 106 years. The kitchen is still the same room--a partition or two has been added and most of the furniture is different. The bedroom where Frank and Annie died is still a bedroom. Unpretentious, antique, at least half-forgotten by the workaday world which speeds south each morning in $20,000-cars, the original Huntsville Baptist Church lacks not for charm and history. Sula, 68, invites her visitor in and explains most of what is known now of the family she married into about 1935:

> His parents were Robert and Carrie McGhee. I met them--Anne and Frank--in 1929, elderly then. Frank married three times. But he separated from the first wife within a year or so. The second wife (some think her name was Ann) gave Frank three children. We figured they married in 1870. There was Joseph, 1872; Mittie N. (Fuller), 1874; Nannie N. (Burt), (1876-1976). Anne, his last wife, gave him two others--Page, 1883, and David, 1885, and 64 years of companionship.[16] I helped take care of them. Uncle Frank became blind in his left eye. Here's a picture of them about 1940. His usual breakfast was three eggs, sausage, pork, or ham (any part of a hog), cornbread and two cups of coffee. About 8:00 a.m. he'd walk in to Oxford and often spend the day. Annie or I would pack him a lunch or he'd buy his food. His hangout was the SAVE-A-PENNY grocery on Cottage Street. He did this even in the 1940s. He caught a ride to town the Saturday before he was taken sick. He had a paralysis in the throat. The last week he couldn't eat. Here's his cane. The tape's where he fixed it from breaking. He sometimes swung it on the dirt (mud) daubers, swatting them to kill 'em in mid flight.

In her April 8, 1980, letter from Oxford, Mrs. Cornelia H. Broadie, a neighbor, asserts: "I knew Uncle Frank all my life. He liked string beans, corn, collards, tomatoes and cornbread. Pork was his favorite meat. He was a very religious and active worshiper in the Huntsville Baptist."

According to his February 27, 1928, soldier's application for pension (he would begin getting it late in 1928 and by 1946 it would be raised to $26.25 a month),[17] Frank was a servant to Capt. Richard P. Taylor of Co. G, 30th North Carolina State Troops, as of September 7, 1861, and remained in that capacity until January 1865. One of his most remarkable achievements was living in the same community for 110 years and dying within some 7,500 feet of his birthplace to the southwest of his home. His two-inch-long obituary in the September 24, 1946, *Oxford Public Ledger* states that he once was sold as a slave at the Granville County courthouse door in Oxford. Though he did not

---

[16]Frank and Anne's ages aggregated to 215 years, comparable to the 217 years of another couple born in slavery who later lived in Hinton, Okla.--Albert Ray, Sr. (Dec. 18, 1838-Mar. 20, 1948) of Co. G, 44th U.S.C.T., and Mary C. Ward Ray (May 3, 1838-Jan. 17, 1946).

[17]McGhee's pension was comparable to the pension of Alfred T. Blackburn, North Carolina's last Civil War veteran.

attend Confederate reunions, Uncle Frank McGhee was among the final ten Tarheel Boys in Gray.

Robert Wilson, who was born January 13, 1836, has remained one of those figures around whom an element of mystery persists, for relatively little is known of him, especially of his youth. This ancient Boy in Gray deserves more space than he will get, since he apparently had no relatives, or close friends knowledgeable on his life yet living in the late 1970s. But "Uncle Bob," as he was familiarly greeted, truly belongs right here. Records show beyond dispute that he was born in slavery in Richmond, Virginia, almost two months before the Battle of the Alamo. Like many a Negro brother, out of loyalty he joined the Army of Northern Virginia to be near his master, a Confederate captain. While it is altogether probable that he witnessed skirmishing actions, perhaps even a battle, served on burial details, and lived some of man's darkest hours, we shall never know the full extent of his service. It appears likely that his captain did not survive the war. We do not know whether Uncle Bob stayed on after the war and worked for his Virginia benefactor. Did he ever have a family of his own? We can say only that he lived right. Six-to-one, he was religious, kind, considerate, and rather quiet and hard-working.[18]

It is known that he lived in Chicago until early 1941. That February, Wilson was admitted at Elgin State Hospital, Elgin, Illinois. Not too many of us are admitted to a hospital at age 105 and stay on for seven-and-a-half years. Perhaps it is just as well we don't, with room rates and fees so out of hand as they are. Although his 112th birthday was celebrated with a big cake and party, Uncle Bob's best gift was a fifty-cent piece sent by Gov. Dwight H. Green to replace a similar coin the governor had given him during a tour of the hospital five years before. The first coin having been "for tobacco," Uncle Bob had refused to spend it, for he proudly displayed it to visitors. Having lost it a few weeks prior to his 112th anniversary, he had become disconsolate; hence, his elation.

At this age he still read his Bible daily. Although this old soldier seems long to have been out of touch with any of his Gray comrades,

---

[18]Possibly a factor in the longevity of so many of the last body servants and mid-20th century ex-slaves was their outdoor physical lifestyle. "Eldest and Last Living Ex-Slaves of the 20th Century," *Last Boys in Gray*, lists at least twenty-two aged blacks who lived to be 120 or more years.

there was, providentially, a certain kindliness attending his last rites. John W. Nelson, Service Officer at the hospital, expressed it best: "It seemed appropriate to bury him in the grounds he had enjoyed so much the last seven years of his life." On account of his having served in the Confederate Army, he could not be buried in a United States military cemetery. So then, that day, April 13, 1948, the *Elgin Daily Courier-News* printed: "Funeral services for Robert (Uncle Bob) Wilson, 112-year-old Negro veteran of the Confederate Army, were held at the Elgin State Hospital at 10:30 this morning. Burial took place in the institution's cemetery." Is it not akin to a spiritual triumph that Wilson was mustered in for this last occasion to be with his buddies, these forty-six years after?

Lewis Carter, born September 10, 1849, was a body servant in the War for the Defense of Virginia. His services were entirely within state and the usual ones described in Bell I. Wiley's *Southern Negroes, 1861-1865*: taking care of his soldier-master's horse, cooking, cleaning clothing, digging earthworks, trenches or graves. It was after 1930 when he finally applied for and began to receive a small pension based upon his military services. In fact, had he not "surfaced" on April 4, 1980, in the "AFTER 1930" card bundles of Virginia Confederate pensioners, the writer undoubtedly never would have discovered him.

Of all Virginia's last War Between the States veterans, Lewis Carter, categorically, was the least glorified, the least publicized, the least known. Even though he was one of the last five Confederates in the Old Dominion, he went to his grave an unknown to these ranks. As to publicity, he sought little and got little. Hence, the writer's own satisfaction in giving Lewis Carter his due place and space here. Lewis was still a boy at his service time. Learning the details of his life has been met with limited success. After ten inquiries, only one response came close to being helpful. A Mrs. Pearl Wallace of Toano, Virginia, offered: "Lewis Carter had a daughter, Rose Coleman, a cousin of mine." Rose Coleman was the informant on her father's death certificate.[19] From this document we also learn that Mary Burrell Carter was Lewis's mother, that his hometown was Lanexa, New Kent County, east of Richmond. His residence and small acreage were just outside of town on Rural Route 1, where he picked up his mail in Box #42.

---

[19]Death Certificate, State File No. 18701, Reg. No. 7-633b, Aug. 30, 1949.

Lewis Carter was a day laborer, working until late in his life. He died at home at 10:20 a.m. of chronic myocarditis (heart disease). The family physician, a Dr. Franklin of West Point, Virginia, had last seen him that May. Lewis came within living until his 100th birthday. He was buried on August 30, 1949, in St. Luke's Cemetery near Lanexa and Plum Point. He died, possibly, in the knowledge that he was one of the nation's last handful of Civil War veterans. Although there were relatively few body servants in service by April 1865, he could well have been one who witnessed Lee's surrender and the stacking of arms. We will never know. Today we render a passing salute, even though he may likely lie in an unmarked grave and just as likely may rest there without any flag.

The last actual personality known to have performed as a body servant, in the usual sense of the term, for the C. S. A. was Hamptonville, Yadkin County, North Carolina's "Uncle Teen" Blackburn. His place in American and Confederate history is solid, for he was for over nine months the Old North State's lone surviving Confederate veteran following the demise of Samuel N. Bennett of Relief, who had served as a youthful private in Company K, 25th North Carolina Infantry, and died March 8, 1951, at age 100 years, 10 months, and 4 days.[20] When "Uncle Teen" finally "got done," he left an even score of Civil War veterans.[21]

Born April 26, 1842, Blackburn was one of some 250 slaves employed on the estates of the Hampton and Cowles Families. With nineteen antebellum years, Teen held vivid memories of those early yuletide holidays, when the two families would each place a huge oak log in their spacious fireplaces and festively celebrate as long as the logs lasted, usually three full days. Having always been dealt with fairly, young Teen was glad enough to go along to the war with his assigned soldier. The timing of that assignment came in early January 1862, when Col. W. H. H. Cowles had Teen accompany his son-in-law, 2nd Lt. Augustus W. Blackburn. Then he shortly repaired directly to Camp Mangum near Raleigh to train with Company B, 38th North Carolina Infantry, commanded by Major J. J. Iredell.

---

[20]"Sam Bennett was 13 years 6-1/2 months on enlistment, but gave his age as 16, having already trained hard with a home guard group at Burnsville. But the lad was only following family, for his grandfather Pitman Williams (52 on enlistment) and three uncles (Pitman's sons, Samuel and William, besides James Bennett) had all joined up in July 1861 with the 29th N. C. Infy." Jay S. Hoar, *Callow Brave and True: A Gospel of Youth in War.*

[21]*Last Boys in Gray*, 33-35.

Teen was just nineteen and already legendary for his ox-like strength. He became Lieutenant Blackburn's personal bodyguard, cook, and helper. It is also believed that at times Teen helped a number of other soldiers of the 38th North Carolina through much of their service in the A.N.V. These two gave steady and vigorous service in Virginia for upwards of two years, until Captain Blackburn, wounded and weakened, reluctantly gave in and allowed himself to be furloughed back to Hamptonville either to recuperate or to die early. Thus, toward the close of hostilities, Teen was already back where he had grown up. The families there were ever after highly appreciative of Teen's own contributions. Perhaps Uncle Teen's favorite story of all was of the time he took up a sword, drew it against an oncoming Yankee, and thus surely saved the life of Captain Blackburn at Second Manassas.[22]

With peace restored, Teen found work on farms. Soon, however, he began carrying the mails by foot, from Hamptonville to Statesville, way south into Iredell County, and he walked this route for forty years. Then for another twenty years he carried the mail from Yadkinville to Jonesville, off to the northwest; but on this route, most of the time, he regaled in the luxury of a mule (or horse) and buggy. It is evident that walking great distances on a frequent basis was a decided factor in keeping his circulatory system in top condition; this very thing was one of the great "secrets" of his longevity and of so many of his fellow body servants. In the meantime, while still a young man, he had married Lucy Carson of Hamptonville. They raised four sons and three daughters and shared some seventy matrimonial years. Their home was on the north-south Statesville-Elkin highway near Hamptonville. He lived at Hamptonville for over a century.

It is said that Teen Blackburn walked daily to Mr. G. C. Wallace's Store, which Teen called "town," to pick up his newspaper, *The Yadkin Ripple*, and sometimes to buy a plug of tobacco. He also enjoyed reading *The Progressive Farmer* magazine. It is also said that his children repaid their father's labors by becoming upstanding citizens: schoolteachers, principals, mail carriers, one becoming a policeman in Washington (Beaufort County). One of the great centers of their lives was Flat Rock Baptist Church, the oldest in Yadkin County.

---

[22] *Yadkin* (Yadkinville, N. C.) *Ripple*, Dec. 20, 1951.

Something of a local sage, he was known widely for his wisdom and humility and for the ability to look into the future. Whenever somebody was sick, he was one of the first in the community to stay up nights with the afflicted.[23] There was, too, about Uncle Teen a buoyant charm that "came through" in a disarming number of ways. This truth is reflected in what Lewis S. Brumfield, a genealogical researcher of Yadkinville, came across recently: Teen's 1941 income tax return, whereon he listed his occupation as "Confederate Soldier (Retired)."[24]

Having been a body servant, Uncle Teen qualified for a Class B Confederate (state) pension of $26.26 monthly. At least North Carolina recognized and rewarded her body servants. The Federal government gave them nothing until it was too late, 1953! However, these veterans were awarded by their respective state governments a final recognition: $100 for burial expenses, the same as for Class-A Confederate veterans. A devout Christian and of jolly disposition, Uncle Teen was one of the Old North State's last known citizens who had been a slave. He was a Class-A American. Like so many Old Rebs and Old Reb body servants before him, Uncle Teen Blackburn, Yadkin County's eldest citizen at the time, went down in the grand manner. He died in his own house in his own bed, the ultimate poem.[25]

Senior Americans today yet fondly remember the aged body servants who were the rearguard of their inimitable folk-type, even those who so naturally came by that redeeming gift called neighborliness. The strenuous life of the Confederate soldier-cavalryman afforded few comforts within the necessarily severe and often abruptly changing military setting. The sheer presence of a few body servants often imparted for the homesick Gray a semblance of normalcy, of the much missed life and family back home. They were walking morale-boosters and sometimes purveyors of needed humor and entertainment. Within the Confederate Army, body servants were a practical and splendid societal component. They aided and abetted the soldiery and their cavalry. As paramilitaries they were

---

23 Marcellene Blackburn Lindsay (granddaughter?), *Yadkin County History*, 115. Precise source of this write-up is not apparent, but photos of Teen at age 108 and of Ann Blackburn (daughter?) are featured.

24 My thanks to Charles Kelly Barrow for sharing this incident mentioned in a March 6, 1994, letter written to Barrow by George W. Wright, Esq., of Teaneck, N. J. Also, my appreciation to J. H. Segars for forwarding the letter to me.

25 *Last Boys in Gray*, 461-62.

"UNCLE TEEN" BLACKBURN AT 107
Author's collection

nonpareil. Looking back at their heyday some thirteen decades ago, perhaps for us today the old-time body servant might seem a somewhat quaint concept. After all, they were a proud and distinctive Southern folk-type who blossomed of necessity, who served courageously, who endured long and faded slowly from the passing scene of American life, until they finally vanished nearly fifty years ago.

NEWSPAPER ACCOUNTS

During the Civil War era, newspapers flourished. The survival of many of these newspapers renders these accounts a veritable "gold mine" for researchers. Early in the war, the southern press reported southern blacks volunteering for military service and conducting benefits to raise funds for the war effort. Later, reports concerned servant-soldiers who tended the wounded, worked on fortifications, and performed a variety of duties, including firing weapons at Union troops. As the fortunes of the Confederacy declined, editorials called for formal recruitment and arming of slaves. Debate over this issue is seen in letters to the editor and in feature articles. Newspaper accounts comprise one of the most readily available sources of the black Confederate experience, as the following examples, reprinted and presented in chronological order, illustrate.

"Tender of the Services of a Company of Negroes"[1]

We are informed that Mr. G. C. Hale, of Autauga County, yesterday tendered to Governor [A. B.] Moore the services of a company of negroes, to assist in driving back the horde of abolition sycophants who are now talking so flippantly of reducing to a conquered province the Confederate States of the South. He agrees to command them himself, and guarantees that they will do effective service. What will our Black Republican enemies think of such a movement as this? We have frequently heard the slaves who accompanied their masters to the "scene of action," assert that when fighting was to be done, they wanted to shoulder their muskets and do their share of it, and we do not have a shadow of a doubt but what they would be found perfectly reliable. An idea seems to have prevailed at the North, that in the event of a war between the two sections, the slaves would become rebellious. Let them no longer lay this flattering unction to their souls. It will avail them nothing.

---

[1] From the *Montgomery Advertiser,* reprinted in the *Southern* (Athens, Ga.) *Banner,* May 1, 1861.

"A Brave Negro"[2]

In the recent battle at Belmont, Lieutenant Shelton, of the 18th Arkansas regiment, had his servant Jack in the fight. Both Jack and his master were wounded, but not till they had made most heroic efforts to drive back the insolent invaders. Finally, after Jack had fired at the enemy *twenty-seven* times, he fell seriously wounded in the arm. Jack's son was upon the field, and loaded the rifle for his father, who shot at the enemy *three times* after he was upon the ground. Jack's son hid behind a tree, and when the enemy retreated they took him to Cairo and refused to let him return. Jack was taken from the field in great pain, and brought to the Overton Hospital, where he bore his sufferings with great fortitude till death relieved him of his pains yesterday. His example may throw a flood of light upon the fancied philanthropy of Abolitionism.

"Donations to the Confederate Cause"[3]

We notice in many of our exchanges that the *colored gentry* of several of the cities of the Confederacy, have displayed much loyalty and patriotism in their donations to the Confederate cause. Balls have been resorted to in a great many instances, from the proceeds of which liberal donations have been made. We are no advocate of this plan to raise the wind, by which our colored gentry display their liberality and loyalty. But as it appears to be tolerated and commended every where, we do not see any good reason why the "colored folks" of Atlanta may not be heralded as having been engaged in the good work, as well as those of other cities. Hence we notice that in ourown goodly city, under the management of Col. Lathum's (of Campbell County) servant, in the employ of the Bank of Fulton in this place, Austin Wright, three of these balls have been given--from two of which twenty dollars have been patriotically contributed for the relief of the families of indigent soldiers, and from a third, fifteen dollars have been contributed to the families of those darkies who are also absent in the service. The balls, of course, were conducted with all due decorum, attended with that variegated display, which is common on all similar occasions!!

---

[2]From the *Memphis Avalanche*, reprinted in the *Daily* (Columbus, Ga.) *Sun*, Nov. 26, 1861.

[3]*Daily* (Atlanta, Ga.) *Intelligencer*, Dec. 28, 1861.

"Soldier's Discharge"[4]

To all Whom it may Concern,

Know Ye, That Charles Benger, a colored Musician of Captain Geo. S. Jones' company, Macon Volunteers 2nd Ga Battalion, who was enlisted the 1st day of May, one thousand eight hundred and sixty-one, to serve one year is hereby honorably discharged from the Army of the Confederate States. Charlie is a patriotic and faithful negro, and deserves good treatment at the hands of any and every Southerner.

Said Charles Benger was born in Camden county in the State of Georgia, is 68 years of age, 5 feet 11 inches high, black complexion, black eyes, grey hair, and by occupation when enlisted a fifer.

Given at Petersburg, Va., this 22d day of July, 1862.

GEO. S. JONES, Capt Macon Vol's
CHARLES J. MOFFETT, Capt. Com'd 2d Ga. Batt., Ga. Vols.

Transportation furnished in kind to Macon, Ga.
E.B. BRANCH, Capt. & A. Qr. M. I. C. S.

"Patriotism among the Colored Population"[5]

We learn that a negro woman, wishing to go "in the war," dressed herself in the uniform of a soldier and went off with the Macon Light Artillery. She was arrested in Augusta and lodged in jail.

---

[4]*Macon* (Ga.) *Daily Telegraph,* July 28, 1862.

[5]From the *Macon Daily Telegraph,* reprinted in the *Columbus* (Ga.) *Daily Sun,* Aug. 1, 1862.

SOLDIER'S DISCHARGE.

To all Whom it may Concern.

Know Ye, That Charles Benger, a colored Musician of Captain Geo. S. Jones' company, Macon Volunteers 2nd Ga. Battalion, who was enlisted the 1st day of May, one thousand eight hundred and sixty-one, to serve one year is hereby honorably discharged from the Army of the Confederate States. Charlie is a patriotic and faithful negro, and deserves good treatment at the hands of any and every Southerner.

Said Charles Benger was born in Camden county in the State of Georgia, is 68 years of age, 5 feet 11 inches high, black complexion, black eyes, grey hair, and by occupation when enlisted, a fifer.

Given at Petersburg, Va., this 22d day of July, 1862. GEO. S. JONES,

CHARLES J. MOFFETT, Capt Macon Vol's.

Capt. Com'd 2d Ga. Batt., Ga. Vols.

Transportation furnished in kind to Macon, Ga. E. B. BRANCH,

Capt. & A. Qr. M. I. C. S.

Journal & Messenger copy.

DISCHARGE NOTICE FOR CHARLES BERGER

From the Macon Daily Telegraph, July 28, 1862

★ THE FORGOTTEN CONFEDERATES ★

P. CHARLES LUNSFORD

JUST AFTER THE TURN OF THE CENTURY, MISS MILDRED Lewis Rutherford, Historian General of the United Daughters of the Confederacy, perhaps the greatest defender of the Old South, said that the "truths of history" would vindicate the memory of our ancestors. Nothing else was necessary. "Miss Milly" was right. All of the adjectives in the world cannot withstand one simple truth.

Our southern ancestors would be particularly perplexed today if they were to witness the recent attacks on everything Confederate. Their reaction would be, simply, to propose a truth that would refute the attack. The thesis consistent in most recent attacks follows that the Confederacy was created to protect and to defend the evil practice of slavery; therefore, the Confederacy was inherently racist. The justification used by most attackers is the latter activities of modern day hate groups who improperly exploit Confederate symbols. Their theory is that Confederates acted against blacks just because of their race.

Aside from the obvious fact that Southerners for years disliked equally Carpetbaggers, "Yankees," and Republicans, regardless of their races, there is a simple truth that eloquently refutes the thesis used against our ancestors. It is a little known truth; nevertheless, it is factual: The overwhelming majority of blacks during the War Between the States supported and defended with armed resistance the cause of southern independence, as did Native Americans, Hispanic Americans, and other minorities. In his book *Blacks in Blue and Gray*, H. C. Blackerby demonstrates that over three hundred thousand blacks, both free and slave, supported the Confederacy, far more than the number that supported the Union.

Today, owing to the lack of extant documentary records, we have a great difficulty in identifying these black Confederates. We must depend upon the work of researchers, such as Blackerby, to give us reliable statistical data. Occasionally, however, information

---

P. Charles Lunsford is an official with the Office of Consumer Affairs, State of Georgia, and a national speaker on southern heritage issues.

emerges that goes far toward enlightening the issue. Such information is in the form of old United Confederate Veterans records, which have revealed the stories of two of the most beloved Confederate veterans in the Atlanta area. Incidentally, both of these veterans were black men.

They were among the most beloved of the veterans. They were cared for extremely well and were featured at U.C.V. reunions for many years. Two surviving programs of U.C.V. reunions in Georgia indicate a number of them present. For example, the reunion of 1905 listed "colored" veterans George Wallace, James Ferguson, Henry Allen, Jerry May, and Frank Hubbard. The program mentioned that all had seen active service, and that all proudly wore their U.C.V. badges. As late as 1933, the U.C.V. reunion program still listed two black members present: Cicero Finch and Bill Yopp; the latter being a member of the Atlanta Camp #159, U.C.V., which met on the third Monday of each month at the State Capitol.

William H. "Ten Cent Bill" Yopp truly was a beloved veteran. He was born in a small slave cabin in Laurens County, Georgia. His master's family was one of the most prominent in the area, producing several members of the state legislature and one member of the Georgia secession convention of 1861. At the age of seven, Bill was bound as a body servant to young T. M. Yopp. The two boys were inseparable. They went everywhere together and became lifelong friends.

When the war broke out, T. M. Yopp, commissioned as a captain in Company H, 14th Georgia Infantry, promptly went to Virginia. Along with him went "Ten Cent Bill." During the many battles of the Army of Northern Virginia, Bill was always by his master's side, twice nursing him back to health from severe wounds. Bill guarded the captain's belongings and consistently found needed provisions. In addition, he served as drummer for the company. When Captain Yopp was wounded at the Battle of Seven Pines, it was Bill who cleaned the wound and nursed the captain back to health. At the Battle of Fredricksburg, Captain Yopp was again severely wounded, and Bill was right there to care for him until, owing to exhaustion, he was sent home. Nevertheless, Bill soon rejoined his master in Virginia and remained at his side until the end of the war. He witnessed the surrender of the Army of Northern Virginia in April 1865.

BILL YOPP

As the outcome of the war became clear, slavery ended. During the earliest days of reconstruction, Bill set out to travel and to earn a living. Yet, many years later, Bill returned to the captain's family. In time, he came to care for his former master at the Georgia Confederate Soldiers' Home in Atlanta. While at the home, Bill gained the love and respect of the other veterans. He was admitted to the Atlanta U.C.V. camp and was prominent at all activities. His relationship with the home's chairman of the board of trustees, Col. R.D. Lawrence, was warm and longlasting.

Bill was very effective in raising funds for the home. For several years he, with the help of the *Macon Telegraph,* raised enough money to give each veteran in the home a gift of $3.00 at Christmas. A book written by Bill concerning his exploits before, during, and after the war was also used for many years as a fundraiser for the home. The veterans at the home were so thankful that they took up a collection in 1920 to have a medal made for Bill, and the board of trustees voted to allow him to stay at the home as long as he lived. For years Bill was an attraction at both the soldiers' home and at the state fair on the day reserved for blacks who fought for and supported the Confederacy. He was one of the last surviving veterans in the home, which closed its doors to veterans in the 1940s.

At the age of 92, Captain Yopp died. Bill was the featured speaker at the memorial service, and it was a particularly emotional one. Not long afterward, Bill joined his longtime friend in the Confederate Cemetery in Marietta, Georgia, where several residents of the home were interred. Clearly, there was not a more beloved veteran than Bill Yopp.

For those who believe the story of "Ten Cent Bill" an anomaly, there's the story of an equally beloved black veteran from another Atlanta U.C.V. camp. It is perhaps the most amazing story of love shown by the old veterans for one of their black compatriots. It is the story of Amos Rucker of Elbert County, Georgia.

Amos went to war with his young master, Col. Sandy Rucker, of the 33rd Georgia Infantry. He was a body servant, at first showing prowess in the procurement of needed supplies when no one else could. There was always a chicken cooking on Colonel Rucker's campfire, no matter how scant the provisions were. Amos did not remain a body servant, however. Soon he found himself in the thick of battle. He was a brave soldier, as he picked up the bayoneted musket of a dead member of his unit and charged the enemy line. He continued performing as a combat soldier for the remainder of the war. Attached to the staff of Gen. Patrick Cleburne, he became the servant of General Cleburne's first cousin, D. C. J. Cleburne. Amos Rucker's duty was to call the roll after each battle, and he committed to memory the entire company. But Amos was not merely a roll caller. Before the surrender, he received a severe wound to his left breast, and a leg wound left him permanently crippled.

After the war Amos joined the W. H. T. Walker Camp U.C.V. in Atlanta. On the second Monday of each month, he faithfully attended the camp's meetings at 102 Forsyth Street. Proud to show his excellent memory, he often recited the names of every member of his old company, from "A to Z." It is said that he solemnly added after each name "here" or "dead."

Amos always said that "My folks give me everything I want." It was true. The members of the camp provided well for Amos, even helping him to acquire a house on the west side of Atlanta. His attorney for the real estate transaction and for the settlement of his estate, as well as for the care of his dear wife, Martha, was John M. Slaton, a member of the John B. Gordon Camp #46, Sons of Confederate Veterans. (Later, as governor of Georgia, Slaton commuted the death sentence of Leo Frank.) Old Amos was a fixture at veterans' meetings; he never missed one until just before his death, when he sent a message to the members: "Give my love to the boys."

His death on August 10, 1905, brought universal sorrow to Atlanta. His body lay in state, while hundreds of Atlantans representing many of the best families of the city silently paid their respects. The members of Camp Walker took care of all funeral expenses and bought a plot for Rucker and his wife at Southview Cemetery, where, today, members of the Martin Luther King family are buried. Funeral services were conducted by Clement A. Evans of Atlanta, Confederate General and U.C.V. Commander-in-Chief. Amos's pallbearers were Gov. Allen D. Candler, Gen. A. J. West, Judge William Lowndes Calhoun, Jr., ex-Postmaster Amos Fox, Frank A. Hilburn, Commander of Camp Walker, J. Sid Holland and R. S. Ozburne, Confederate veterans all.

An article in the *Confederate Veteran* related the sadness: "Very tenderly they carried the old veteran to his grave, clothed in his uniform of gray and wrapped in a Confederate flag, a grave made beautiful by flowers from comrades and friends, among which a large design from the Daughters of the Confederacy was conspicuous in its red and white." The Rev. Dr. T. P. Cleveland led the prayer, and several of Amos's favorite songs were sung. Just before the casket was lowered into the ground, Capt. William "Tip" Harrison read a poem entitled "When Rucker Called the Roll." There was not a dry eye in the place, including his former master, D. C. J. Cleburne, and the son of General Cleburne, Dr. Ronaryne Cleburne, who had made the trip to Atlanta for the services.

Today, the fine stone placed in 1909 by the U.C.V. is gone and the grave of the most beloved of black veterans is barren. Both Amos and his dear Martha lie side-by-side, almost forgotten. Only the sexton's map identifies the spot. It is as if someone did not want us to know about poor old Amos.

In fact, it may well be that there are hundreds of similar stories, now lost. It is our duty, however, to bring them to light. Our southern ancestors were as loyal and as loving to those of their own race as any ever were, black or white. The stories of "Ten Cent Bill" Yopp and Amos Rucker are clear reminders. And we will not forget.

OBITUARIES & BIOGRAPHICAL SKETCHES

The deaths of old black Confederates were at one time recognized and celebrated community events, as the following examples clearly illustrate.

"Uncle Gilbert is Dead"[1]

The casual hearer will say what of that! More than any other old worn negro but to a Confederate Veteran what a train this simple announcement sets in motion. On a spring day in 1861 the first company of the bright young manhood of Newton County marched through the streets of Covington to board a train bound for Richmond, the seat of War and capitol of our young Confederacy.

At their head marched Gilbert Carter, their fifer playing perhaps "The Girl I Left Behind Me." Their banner floated proudly in the rippling Southern breeze. They made a brave picture of Georgia chivalry. They left with the blessings of old men and the prayers and tears of mothers, wives and sisters. This was but the beginning of the sacrifice that was in store for the South. How many of these young men found graves along the rivers and in the valleys of Virginia. The records alone can tell. But in the providence of God their faithful black fifer has been permitted to reach nearly the century mark.

Uncle Gilbert was a typical representative of the faithful slave and they deserve a monument at our hands. He gave obedience to his master and diligently performed the task he was given to do. In the Army he was a great help to the boys, frequently cheering the heart of some homesick youth who found the hardship of camp very different from the romance of war. After he became a free man he deported himself quietly and was respectful to everyone setting a good example to his race and as long as he was able earned his work. . . . At one time he was the servant of Howell Cobb, thus we see he came in contact with the representative white people of Georgia and received great benefit thereby and as a free man he associated with

---

[1]From *The* (Covington, Ga.) *Enterprise*, Jan. 18, 1907.

the best element of his race and always commended obedience to the law and peace between the races. At the time of his death he is said to have been 99 years old. He was buried in Covington, January 13, 1907 by the colored masons. The sun was shining brightly. The evening was as pleasant as a summer day and as the services were ended the sun went behind the western hills, the great crowd of whites and blacks who attended his funeral quietly dispersed to their homes conscious of the fact that they had paid the last tribute of respect to a faithful slave, a quiet and industrious free man and a good friend."

"A Negro Man Honored by All Darlingtonians"[2]

There was a funeral in Darlington Sunday afternoon which whites and blacks attended in almost equal numbers. There were many ladies in the church and the pallbearers were 12 of the leading white citizens of the town, headed by Hon. C. J. McCullough, mayor. The Darlington Guards acted as honorary escorts and the Rev. D. M. Fulton, pastor of the Presbyterian Church conducted the services, assisted by the Rev. J. J. Jefferson of the Colored Presbyterian Church. A large, representative concourse followed the remains from the humble little home to the grave and when the last words were spoken the bugler of the Darlington Guards sounded "taps" and the soldiers fired a salute of three rounds over the still form in the newly made grave.

And this, in brief, is the story of the funeral of Henry Brown, a negro man. In his life he has been true to all--white and black--and when the end came there were many sorrowing ones who were saddened at this death of a good man, whose name has here been a household word for generations.

Henry Brown, familiarily and affectionately known as "old Uncle Dad Brown," died at his home here Saturday evening. . . . Henry was never a slave but came to Darlington from Camden when he was quite a little child. For more than 80 years he lived his life here and his

---

[2]From the obituary of Henry Brown, as extracted from *The* (Columbia, S.C.) *State*. Brown's headstone reveals his date of death as having been November 2, 1907.

character and his deeds proclaimed, in no uncertain tones, the spirit that animated him. . . .

Henry was a veteran of three wars and he had more to say concerning the experiences on the field than in other things, but his best work was not done when he was a follower in the Mexican, Civil nor Spanish-American wars. He had a hard battle to fight for principle and right, but his honest old heart was as brave as it was true and he never faltered for one moment. He was a "Red-shirt-'76 Democrat" of the most patriotic variety and he was a Democrat, not from hope of reward, but one from his heart. . . . His influence was marked among the negroes. He differed with them honestly and told them so squarely. . . .

Henry Brown was a man of rare true worth. He was honored in life and he was honored by last tribute paid to him. It is more than probable that a suitable monument will soon be erected to the memory of one who stood firm in his faith and manhood always, and who, in his humble sphere, met life's problems with the quiet courage that enabled him to live in accordance with the principles that stood inviolate under all circumstances.

Obituary Notice for Calvin Scruggs[3]

Calvin Scruggs, aged negro and life long resident of this city, died yesterday morning at his home on Madison Street after an illness of several months.

His passing marks the almost complete obliteration of the old war time negroes and faithful servitors of the families, some of whom have long been mere names in this community.

Born about 1845, he was reaching manhood at the time of the War Between the States and took part in the local turmoil.

His reminiscences of those battle-torn days were exact and colorful. Birth and circumstances made him a slave without the bonds of slavery, and during the period of reconstruction, where all slaves

---

[3]Scruggs was born on a plantation in Madison County, Alabama. His obituary appeared in *The Huntsville Times*, Aug. 31, 1929.

were freed, he chose to cast his lot in with that of the family to which he had previously belonged, and to which he remained faithful until his death.

His loss will be regretted by members of Huntsville's older families who admired and respected him.

Obituary Notice for Charles Richardson[4]

Funeral service for Uncle Charles Richardson, 95, negro slave and veteran of the Confederate army, will be held Thursday afternoon at 3 o'clock from the colored Methodist Church. . . . He drew a Confederate pension, having fought through the war with his young master who was killed, and later supplied money to take his second master, a Confederate officer and himself to St. Louis.

---

[4]From the *Arkansas* (Little Rock) *Democrat*, Apr. 24, 1929.

CONFEDERATE DRUMMER HENRY BROWN
Courtesy Darlington Historical Commission

JERRY W. MAY, CONFEDERATE VETERAN, WHO DIED IN 1905

The *Atlanta Journal* of Aug. 20, 1990, featured an article about a gravesite memorial service held for this veteran, with the headlines: "Group honors ex-slave who became black rebel, Confederate heirs see no irony in tribute." At the memorial service Confederate reenactors presented a twenty-one-gun salute, while Sons of Confederate Veterans officials paid their tributes as well. "We're not honoring this man because he is black," remarked one of the memorialists. "We're honoring him because he was a Confederate soldier."

★ SOUTH CAROLINA'S BLACK CONFEDERATES ★

ALEXIA J. HELSLEY

THE SOUTH CAROLINA CONFEDERATE PENSION APPLICATIONS tendered under the act of 1923 are unique. Although South Carolina provided in 1866 a short-lived disability compensation, and as early as 1887 pension relief was granted for regular Confederate soldiers, the state did not recognize the service of black South Carolinians until 1923. On March 16, 1923, the legislature approved "An Act to Provide Pensions for certain faithful Negroes who were engaged in the service of the State in the War between the States." Under this legislation, any blacks who had served the Confederacy loyally as "servants, cooks or attendants" were eligible for a pension. However, additional qualifications required at least six months of service and the recommendation by the County Board of Pensions. These pensions were not to exceed $25 annually.

Too many blacks applied under the 1923 act, so the following year lawmakers amended the original act to include only South Carolina residents who had served the state for at least six months as "body servants or as male camp cooks." Therefore, the 1924 act eliminated laborers, teamsters, and all others who had not served in South Carolina units.

Although petitions do not exist for all counties, a sizeable body of these applications for pensions is extant. In 1924 the state appropriated $750,000 for white pensions and expended $744,672.85. During this same year the state designated $3,000 for black pensions and $2,840 was expended. It is difficult to ascertain the average per capita expenditure for black pensioners, because the number approved in 1924 is not known. If, however, pensions were not to exceed $25, then there were at least 113 pensioners that year. In 1946 the last appropriation for black pensions was made, but none of the $75 allotted was expended.

Generally, blacks were employed in limited capacities by the Confederate forces. They served primarily as body servants and

---

Adapted from an article courtesy of the South Carolina Department of Archives and History, Columbia.

cooks, but large labor levees were also drawn by the state to build coastal fortifications and to man essential industries. A letter accompanying the application of Ben P. Griffin of Pickens mentions that Griffin had been sent by his master "by the request of Gov. Pickens for labors" to Fort Sumter. The goal of such work forces was to free white men for military service.

The 1923 petitions often give the type and location of service in detail. For example, Louis Pon of Orangeburg "Hauled supplies from Livingston Mill at Beaver Creek for shipment to troops at Charleston." William Hook, also of Orangeburg, constructed breastworks on James Island, Sullivan's Island, and at "Hampton's race track near Columbia." Henry Williams of Greenville "served with Major William Hay at Charleston, South Carolina making salt for distribution among the people of upper South Carolina."

Many of the laborers served in capacities which involved considerable mobility. For example, Benjamin Singleton of Beaufort began his service as a servant to Capt. John H. Thompson and continued with him until Thompson was killed at Second Manassas. Singleton then served in the Beaufort Volunteers under Sgt. William Thompson and Corp. David Thompson, "until after the battle of Honey Hill." Singleton ended the war serving under Robert and James Thompson with the Citadel Cadets and the "Columbia School Boys."

Other applicants for pensions had engaged in specialized service. W. S. Lewis of Charleston was the servant of James Thurston in the marine corps aboard the C.S.S. *Atlanta,* while William Sanders of Barnwell was "Body servant" to Dr. J. B. Baxley, "a surgeon in the army in charge of the Third Georgia Hospital, Augusta, Georgia." Several of the applicants mentioned having been wounded while in Confederate service. For example, J. K. Knight from Oconee was wounded at Petersburg in 1864, and Spencer Copeland of Laurens injured his foot as he was digging on the breastworks at Charleston. The injury was so severe, that his leg had to be amputated.

The applications for Confederate pension contain touching references to the devotion many servants had to their masters. Anthony Watts from Laurens served until his master had died from battle wounds, and then arranged to have the body transported back home. Zack Brown of Fairfield was a body servant to Robert F.

Coleman, until Coleman was injured, whereupon Brown "stayed with him in hospital til it was captured." Jim Hampton of Anderson summed up his service to his master this way: "Samuel Wilkes was killed in July [1862] and I came home with His Body." Wade Childs, also of Anderson, served Captain Cothran in Orr's Rifles. When Cothran was wounded at Second Manassas, Childs, exhibiting great courage, carried him on his back to the rear of the fighting. Only one of the applicants, Tom Bing of Hampton, professed to have served as a "private soulder," in Colcock's Regiment under Capt. Bill Peebles from 1861 to the end of the war. Unfortunately, there is no extant evidence that verifies this claim.

One of the most interesting applications on record was filed by Jacob Washington of Hampton, whose petition contains considerable autobiographical information. Born in 1844, Washington began serving his master "at 12 years old as a House Servant." In 1861 he served his "Boss," Peter Craddock, as a cook and hostler in camp at Pocataligo. However, when Federal forces captured Bay Point and Beaufort, Washington took his "mistress" to refuge. Later, Craddock joined Hampton's Legion, and Washington attended him until Lee's surrender. Afterward, as Washington put it, "we came Home and made a crop on the Place after which we parted and He went to St. Augustine."

Black pension applications contain useful incidental information. Some petitions reveal name changes which took place after emancipation. There are a few indications of the applicants' ages. Some petitions reveal the names of former owners, and there are occasional references to the applicants' health and literacy at the time of application.

Of course, none of these men appear on official muster rolls or in military records. Were it not for their pension applications, the employment and Confederate service of these black South Carolinians would have been lost forever and entirely forgotten.

Joe Sarter of Union, South Carolina, displays the sword his father carried while in Confederate service as a sentry. The Sons of Confederate Veterans held a memorial service and placed a headstone for Alec Sarter on December 11, 1993. *Courtesy Union Daily Times*

CONFEDERATE PENSION APPLICATIONS, U.C.V. CAMP RECORDS, & REUNIONS

Although blacks were never officially mustered into the Confederate military, they nonetheless served in and supported southern units, and their services were often recognized long after the war had ended when various state governments awarded them pensions and other forms of public relief. Moreover, ex-Confederates groups remembered the contributions made by southern blacks to the Cause, by aiding worthy blacks who applied for pensions and treating them as guests of honor at Confederate reunions. The following document all three of these important sources of evidence documenting the wartime experiences of black Confederates.

BLACK CONFEDERATE PENSION APPLICANTS OF TENNESSEE[1]

Name	Regiment	Military Occupation
Akins, John	9th Tenn Cav.	
Allison, Sam	7th Tenn. Cav.	
Amy, Pete		supply wagon driver
Anderson, George	9th Tenn. Cav.	
Anderson, Ike	1st Ky. Cav.	
Arnold, Polk	Forrest's Escort	
Avant, Alfred Scott		
Averitt, Alfred	18th Tenn. Inf.	
Baker, Jim		laborer
Banks, Foster	2nd Tenn. Inf.	
Barksdale, Henderson	12th Tenn. Inf.	
Bates, Henry		
Beaumont, Ben	10th Tenn. Cav.	
Bell, Charles	11th Tenn. Inf.	
Bell, William Carroll	30th Tenn. Inf.	

---

[1] Pension applications from these 267 black Confederates are found on microfilm in the Tennessee State Library and Archives, Nashville.

BLACK PENSION APPLICANTS OF TENNESSEE (cont.)

Name	Regiment	Military Occupation
Bibb, William	12th Ala. Inf.	
Blackwell, Abe		
Bledsoe, William A.	6th Tenn. Inf.	
Bobbitt, Carter	14th Tenn. Cav.	
Boyd, George		
Bradley, R. H.	29th Miss. Inf.	
Brown, Alfred		
Brown, Anderson		horse shoer
Brown, John L.	20th Tenn. Inf.	
Bryant, Henry	"recruit office"	
Buchanan, Henry	12th Tenn. Inf.	
Buford, William	9th Tenn. Inf.	
Burns, Dave	8th Tenn. Cav.	
Caldwell, John	1st Tenn. Cav.	
Cale, Nat		
Cannon, Charles	154th Tenn. Inf.	
Cansler, Hugh Lawson	43rd Tenn. Inf.	
Carter, Bob		
Caruthers, John	48th Tenn. Inf.	
Cason, Frazier	31st Tenn. Inf.	
Catlett, Tom		
Chapman, Toney	4th Tenn. Cav.	
Church, Henry	48th Tenn. Inf.	
Churchill, John		
Clayton, Sam	46th Tenn. Inf.	
Cleveland, Maurice A.		
Coleman, David B.	6th Ala. Inf.	
Coleman, Jacob	11th Ala. Inf.	
Collier, Sam	6th Tenn. Inf.	
Conn, George A.		
Cotton, Alonzo		
Crudy, Henry D.	7th Tenn. Inf.	
Crutcher, Jack	20th Tenn. Inf.	
Cullom, Sam W.	8th Tenn. Inf.	
Cunningham, Osborne	1st Tenn. Cav.	
Dabney, Mack	4th Tenn. Inf.	
Dance, George	8th Tenn. Inf.	
Davis, Ben	Forrest's H.Q.	
DeGraffenseed, Nathan	154th Tenn. Inf.	

BLACK PENSION APPLICANTS OF TENNESSEE (cont.)

Name	Regiment	Military Occupation
Dillon, Jim	47th Tenn. Inf.	
Dismukes, Abraham		shoe man
Donnell, William M.		commissary dept.
Dortch, Charles	2nd Ky. Cav.	
Douglass, Levi		
Drake, G. W.	16th Tenn. Inf.	
Duke, Alfred	3rd Tenn. Cav.	
Duncan, James	1st Tenn. Inf.	
Dunn, James	7th Tenn. Cav.	
Earle, Turner	3rd Tenn. Cav.	
Easley, Edom	10th Tenn. Cav.	
Easley, W. M.	24th Tenn. Inf.	
East, George W.	24th Tex. Cav.	
Elder, Hal		
Farrington, Joe	5th N.C. Cav.	
Fitzgerald, John M.	48th Tenn. Inf.	
Forrest, Thornton	Forrest's H.Q.	steward
Foster, Joe	9th Tenn. Cav.	
Fountain, Willis	6th Miss. Inf.	
Francis, Edward		hospital steward
Fuller, Lee	5th Ala. Cav.	
Garner, George	1st Tenn. Inf.	
Garrett, George W.		
Garrett, Noah		
Gatewood, Wesley	7th Miss. Inf.	
Gentry, James	17th Tenn. Inf.	
Gibson, John		
Gilliam, Robert		
Gober, Silas	3rd Tenn. Cav.	
Gooch, James	4th (McLemore's) Tenn. Cav.	
Gordon, Nathan	11th Tenn. Cav.	
Gore, Henry	8th Tenn. Cav.	
Gray, Albert	24th Tenn. Inf.	
Gray, Dock		
Green, John		
Greer, Jones	Forrest's Escort	
Gregory, Ned	1st Tenn. (Turney's) Inf.	
Grigsby, Thomas R.	15th Tenn. Cav.	
Grimes, Daniel W.	11th Tenn. Inf.	

BLACK PENSION APPLICANTS OF TENNESSEE (cont.)

Name	Regiment	Military Occupation
Griffin, Butler	26th Ga. Inf.	
Hailey, Albert	44th Tenn. Inf.	
Hairston, John		
Hale, Reuben G.	4th Tenn. Inf.	quartermaster dept.
Hanna, George	3rd Tenn. Cav.	
Hannah, Jerry		
Harding, James	9th Tenn. Cav.	
Harris, Wash		
Hastin, J. G.	42nd Ga. Cav.	
Hastings, Alex	17th Tenn. Inf.	
Hawthrone, E. D.	7th Tenn. Cav.	
Hayes, Caesar	154th Tenn. Inf.	
Haynes, Washington	5th Tenn. Inf.	
Hays, Luke		
Henderson, Henry		
Henry, Wes	2nd Tenn. Cav.	
Hickerson, Clay	24th Tenn. Inf.	
Hord, Frederick R.	2nd Tenn. Cav.	
Hornbeak, Rash		
Hunter, Booker		
Inman, Ezekiel	5th Tenn. Cav.	
Ivie, Wiley S.		quartermaster dept.
Jackson, Henry		
Jarnigan, David	16th Tenn. Cav.	
Jennings, Joseph	12th Tenn. Cav.	
Johnson, George F.		
Johnson, Peter		
Johnson, Richard	14th Miss. Inf.	
Johnson, Tom	50th Tenn. Inf.	
Johnson, William		
Jones, B. J.	3rd Tenn. Inf.	
Jones, Leroy	4th Tenn. Inf.	
Jones, Monroe	Miss. Art.	
Jones, Willis		
Jones, Zack	24th Tenn. Inf.	
Kennedy, Manuel	15th Miss. Cav.	
Kennedy, James	46th Tenn. Inf.	
Kinnard, Taylor	54th Tenn. Inf.	
Kirk, Sam		hospital steward

BLACK PENSION APPLICANTS OF TENNESSEE (cont.)

Name	Regiment	Military Occupation
Knight, Louis	17th Tenn. Inf.	
Lacy, George	14th Tenn. Cav.	
Lankford, Archie D.	2nd Tenn. Cav.	
Ledbetter, Ralph	1st Tenn. Inf.	
Lee, Clark		
Lester, Richard	3rd Tenn. Inf.	
Lester, Robert	8th Tenn. Inf.	
Liggett, R. M.	2nd Tenn. Cav.	
Ligon, Henry	14th Tenn. Inf.	
Lipscomb, Thomas	9th Tenn. Btn. Cav.	
Littrell, Charley	14th Tenn. Cav.	
Locke, Alfred	1st Tenn. Cav.	
McCarter, William	62nd Tenn. Inf.	
McClasen, Bob	13th Tenn. Cav.	
McCullough, Ned	17th Tenn. Inf.	
McDowell, Andrew	5th Tenn. Btn. Cav.	
McEwen, George W.	1st Tenn. Inf.	
McFarland, Doll		
McMillan, William	17th Va. Cav.	
McNeal, Sam	7th Tenn. Cav.	
McNeeley, Sam	14th Tenn. Cav.	
McNeely, Rush	27th Tenn. Inf.	
McNeil, Ausburn		teamster
Maclin, James	7th Tenn. Cav.	
Maney, James	1st Tenn. (Field's) Inf.	
Mason, Plink		wagon train driver
Matthewson, George	Ga. Troops	
Mayberry, Jim	24th Tenn. Inf.	
Mayes, Harrison	1st Tenn. Cav.	
Mickles, Stephen	9th Miss. Inf.	
Miller, William	11th Tenn. Cav.	
Minor, Ned	10th Tenn. Cav.	
Moore, Benjamin		
Moore, John	10th Tenn. Cav.	
Moore, Giles	9th Tenn. Cav.	
Morris, Paden		
Morrison, Wyatt		
Moses, John	7th Tenn. Cav.	
Murray, Branch	17th Miss. Inf.	

BLACK PENSION APPLICANTS OF TENNESSEE (cont.)

Name	Regiment	Military Occupation
Murray, Charles	4th Tenn. (Murray's) Cav.	
Musgrove, Billie W.	8th Miss. Cav.	
Muzzall, Lewis	20th Tenn. Cav.	
Neal, Henry		
Nelson, Henry	19th & 20th Tenn. Cav.	
Nelson, Louis	7th Tenn. Cav.	
Newsom,Sam		
Newsom, Silas	20th Tenn. Inf.	
Nicholson, Isaac R.	Polk's Corps	commissary dept.
Nolen, Alex.	14th Tenn. Inf.	
Norris, Bill		
Nowell, Smith	7th Tenn. Cav.	
O'Neal, William	12th Miss. Cav.	
Otey, Ephraim		quartermaster dept.
Parrish, John	2nd Tenn. Cav.	
Patton, Robert B.	4th Tenn. Cav.	
Payne, Fink		
Payne, Tillman Price	4th Tenn. Cav.	
Pearce, George	8th Tenn. Cav.	
Phillips, Asa	1st Tenn. Inf.	
Porter, Alex.	20th Tenn. Cav.	
Pugh, Dawson	7th Tenn. Cav.	
Quarles, Harvey	8th Tenn. Inf.	
Ransom, Alexander	24th Tenn. Inf.	
Read, Henry	7th Tenn. Cav.	
Ready, Albert	23rd Tenn. Inf.	
Reeves, James	7th Tenn. Inf.	
Reid, Nathan	6th Tenn. Inf.	
Rice, Richard	29th Tenn. Inf.	
Rivers, Matt	11th Tenn. Cav.	
Robertson, William		
Robinson, James		
Robison, John O.		
Rodgers, William	31st Tenn. Inf.	
Rowe, Will	2nd. Ky. Cav.	
Rucker, William H.	2nd Tenn. Inf.	
Russell, Frank	Forrest's Escort	
Russell, Peter		
Sanford, Peter		

BLACK PENSION APPLICANTS OF TENNESSEE (cont.)

Name	Regiment	Military Occupation
Schoolfield, H. M.		
Searcy, Shadrick	46th Tenn. Inf.	body servant
Seay, Frank M.	24th Tenn. Inf.	
Sweeney, George W.	14th Miss. Inf.	
Shad, Stephen	10th Tenn. Cav.	
Shayse, Cal		
Shelly, Wallace		hospital steward
Smith, Coleman D.		body servant
Smith, J. Wesley	17th Tenn. Inf.	
Smith, Lewis	16th Tenn. Cav.	
Smith, Presley	6th Tenn. Inf.	
Starnes, Hardin	4th Tenn. Cav.	
Stegall, Robert		quartermaster's dept.
Stephenson, Monroe	9th Tenn. Btn. Cav.	
Stone, Tee		laborer Island No. 10
Stover, Robert		
Swift, Aaron	12th Tenn. Inf.	
Tansie, Ed	31st Tenn. Inf.	
Terry, John		
Thomas, Add		
Thomas, Ben	31st Ala. Inf.	
Thompson, Marshall	4th Tenn. Cav.	
Thornton, Edward		teamster
Tidwell, Marshall	24th Tenn. Inf.	
Travis, Jack	27th Tenn. Inf.	
Tuggle, Richard	13th Tenn. Inf.	
Turner, Peter	30th Tenn. Inf.	
Tyson, Alfred	12th Ky. Cav.	
Vertrees, Peter	6th Ky. Cav.	
Walker, Bailey	13th Tenn. Inf.	
Walker, Isaac L.		
Ward, Mose	24th Tenn. Inf.	
Ware, Charles	16th Tenn. Inf.	
Watkins, Wade	48th Tenn. Inf.	
Webb, Charlie	13th Tenn. Inf.	
Webber, Lee	2nd Ky. Cav.	
Wharton, Big Alex	154th Tenn. Inf.	
Wharton, Little Alex	21st Tenn. Cav.	
Wharton, Frank	14th Tenn. Cav.	

BLACK PENSION APPLICANTS OF TENNESSEE (cont.)

Name	Regiment	Military Occupation
White, Dick	6th Tenn. Inf.	
Whitelow, Wright	Forrest's Cav.	
Whiteside, Charlie	48th Tenn. Inf.	
Wilkerson, Charles	1st Tenn. Cav.	
Wilkes, Nim	Forrest's H.Q.	
Williams, G. H.	18th Tenn. Inf.	
Windrow, Wyatt		
Winfield, Henry		bodyguard
Winston, Maniel	9th Tenn. Inf.	
Withers, James	3rd Miss. Cav.	
Wood, M. E.		
Woods, John		
Woods, Smith	20th Tenn. Cav.	
Word, George	20th Tenn. Cav.	
Wright, Austin	7th Tenn. Cav.	
Wyatt, Billie	3rd Mo. Cav.	
Yansey, George W.	4th Ga. Cav.	
Youree, Henry	2nd Tenn. Cav.	

MINUTES OF THE ZEB VANCE CAMP, U.C.V., HAZELHURST, GA.

The May [1930] meeting of the Zeb Vance Camp of United Confederate Veterans, held in Confederate Hall of the County Court House on the 30th instant, was attended by an unually large number of members on account of plans then formulated for the general reunion to be held in Biloxi, Mississippi June 3-6 inclusive. . . .

A new member received into the Camp was Gilbert Baird a faithful colored man who served the Confederacy during the War Between the States. . . .

BLACK CONFEDERATE PENSIONERS OF NORTH CAROLINA[2]

Name	Owner/Military Occupation
Allen, Henry	laborer hauling supplies
Alston, Isaac	Bill Allen/body servant
Andrews, Andrew	George Mordecai
Ashcraft, Wilson C.	Thomas E. Ashcraft/body servant
Atwater, Alexander	William Stroud/teamster
Baird, Gilbert	James A. Baird
Ballentine, George	Alsie Holland/teamster
Beebe, Sam	body servant
Bennett, John	S. H. Philpott/body guard
Bitttle, John	Wes Biddle/body servant
Bizzell, Agrippe	
Blackburn, Alfred	Capt. Augustus Blackburn/servant
Blackburn, Wiley	Capt. Augustus Blackburn/servant
Cooper, Ed	
Fletcher, Sandy	Sgt. Wm. C. Covington/servant
Howard, Elisha	
Liggins, Will	body servant
Revels, William C.	musician[3]

[2]Extracted from *Wake* (North Carolina Genealogical Society) *Treasures*, (Spring 1992).

[3]Pension records indicate that Revels, who enlisted in Co. H, 21st N.C. Inf., on June 5, 1861, was wounded in the left leg at Winchester, Va., in the right thigh at Gettysburg, and in the right shoulder at New Bern.

BLACK CONFEDERATE PENSIONERS OF YORK COUNTY, S.C.[4]

Name	Served Under
Agurs, Samuel W.	Captain Culp
Banks, Noah	William Avery
Barnett, Anthony	Commander, Sullivan's Island
Barron, Harvey	Commander, Ft. Sumter
Bird, George[5]	J. C. Chambers
Chambers, Anderson	Commander, Ft. Sumter
Crawford, Peter	William Crawford
Guy, Adam	Captain Roberson
Harris, James	William Crosby
Leech, Sam	Commander, Ft. Sumter
Mackey, Jeff	Dr. J. F. Mackey
Marshall, Heyward	Dr. J. Rufus Bratton
Melton, George	Samuel Melton
Smith, Alvin Bratton	D. J. Smith
White, Henry	J. W. White

BLACK CONFEDERATES WHO ATTENDED U.C.V. REUNION IN ARKANSAS (1928)[6]

Name	Residence
Baker, Tom	Tupelo, Miss.
Black, W. M.	Marrianna, Ark.
Boldy, Henry	Boldy, Ala.
Bradley, R. H.	Jackson, Tenn.
Chambers, Professor	Winston, Ark.
Everhardt, Steve	Rome, Ga.
Gray, Mat	Huntsville, Ala.
Hood, Bill	Houston, Tex.
Horthown, "Uncle"	Brownsville, Tenn.

[4] Extracted from Sam Thomas, "Afro-American Confederates in York County," *The* (York County Genealogical and Historical) *Quarterly*.

[5] A free person from Sandersville, S.C., who enlisted in 1861 as a cook in Co. A, 12th South Carolina Volunteers (Palmer Guards), and served throughout the war.

[6] *Arkansas* (Little Rock) *Democrat*, May 11, 1928; *Southwest* (Fort Smith) *Times Record*, May 13, 1928.

BLACK CONFEDERATES WHO ATTENDED U.C.V. REUNION IN ARKANSAS (cont.)

Name	Residence
Lemons, C.C.	Calvert, Tex.
Manuel, Steve	Mark, Miss.
Maple, "Uncle"	Sulphur Springs, Tex.
McConnell, Lewis	College Hill, Ark.
Neely, Rev. H. M.	Columbus, Miss.
Nelson, Louis	Ripley, Tenn.
Phillips, Simon	Birmingham, Ala.
Pringle, Isaac	Meridian, Miss.
Slaughter, W. H.	Culpepper, Va.
Weatherford, H. W.	Arkansas
Winfull, Dan	Sweet Home, Ark.

BLACK CONFEDERATE PENSIONERS OF MARSHALL COUNTY, MISS.[7]

Name	Residence
Arnold, Pud	Byhalia
Boggan, Ben	Byhalia
Bowen, Henry	
Brunson, Jim	Byhalia
Bryon, Adam	
Bruton, Edward	Holly Springs
Dean, Ben	Chulahoma
Dockery, Tom	
Duncan, Ben	Holly Spring
Garrett, Hardy	Holly Spring
Hill, David	Waterford
Hill, Monroe	Holly Springs
Howell, Tobe	
Ingram, Tony	Byhalia
Joyner, William	Mt. Pleasant
Lay, Richard	Waterford
Leggett, Martin	
Lester, Coleman	Holly Springs
Matthews, Manuel	Victoria
McKissack, Norwood	
Peal, Alfred	
Phillips, Fletcher	Chulahoma
Pryor, Adam	Laws Hill
Smith, James	Byhalia
Spears, George	Holly Springs
Walker, Robert	Holly Springs
White, Wyatt N.	
Wilson, Joe	Holly Springs

---

[7]Extracted from *"The Gray Ghost,"* (Holly Springs, Miss.) S.C.V. Camp Newsletter (1991).

Score of Negro War Veterans At Reunion

Former Slaves Who Served With Masters Enjoy Gathering.

There are more than a score of the survivors of the negro veterans who fought with their masters in the Civil war present at the reunion. These grizzled old former slaves find their greatest pleasure in seeing the sons, or "young masters" of the officers they served during the war and of talking over old times with their buddies at the reunion.

The greater number of these negro soldiers, says old "Uncle Steve" Manuel, who served as a groom, camp tender, cook and forager for General (Pap) Price, one of the oldest officers in the war, went with their masters to the front when war was declared. In those days they were all young fellows and considered it the greatest honor to fight for and, with their masters. Many heated arguments as to who was the greatest leader in the war arise among these old fellows quartered at Fair park.

Most of the negro soldiers in the war tended their former masters and the commanding officers' horses, cooked for them, foraged and tended their camps. The old eyes of the negro veterans, which are growing gray with age, brighten up as they tell of the many incidents in the war when their "watermelon and chicken stealing" activities "back home" in their younger days stood them in good stead. The tables of the officers never lacked chicken when they were in enemy territory as long as an expert of that line was in camp.

Known names of the negro veterans present at the reunion are: Steve Manuel of Mark, Miss.; Louis Nelson of Ripley, Tenn.; R. H. Bradley of Jackson, Tenn.; Dan Winfull of Sweet Home, Ark.; W. M. Black of Marrianna, Ark.; the Rev. H. M. Neely of Columbus, Miss.; "Uncle" Horthown of Brownsville, Tenn.; "Uncle" Maple and his wife of Sulphur Springs, Tex.; C. C. Lemons of Calvert, Texas; Isaac Pringle of Meridian, Miss.; W. H. Slaughter of Culpepper, Va.; Simon Phillips of Birmingham, Ala.; Professor Chambers of Winston, Ark.; Mat Gray of Huntsville, Ala.; Henry Boldy of Chase, Ala.; Steve Arerhart of Rome, Ga.; Tom Baker of Tupelo, Miss.; Bill Hood of Houston, Texas; H. W. Weatherford of Arkansas, and there are four or five others whose names have not been ascertained.

Many more survivors of the slaves who fought with their masters in the Civil war are still living, but were unable to attend the reunion here. Nearly everyone of them is a former slave, and each is high in his praise of his "old master" 'way back "befo' de wah."

WHENEVER CONFEDERATE VETERANS REUNITED, THERE WAS A GREAT DEAL OF PUBLICITY, ESPECIALLY WHEN BLACK VETERANS WERE IN ATTENDANCE.
From the Arkansas Democrat, May 11, 1928

REUNION PHOTOGRAPH OF THE 5TH TENNESSEE INFANTRY

Veteran Johnny Orr (#14) passes his blessings to compatriot Hermann Kendall (#41) in the old southern evangelical tradition of "laying on hands." *Courtesy Paris (Tenn.) Post Intelligencer*

CONFEDERATE REUNION IN HUNTSVILLE, ALABAMA (*ca.* 1928)

VETERANS' REMINISCENCES & NARRATIVES

The varied contributions made by blacks to the Confederacy have been remembered and documented in the past. These reminiscences and narratives are among the best sources for the study of black Confederates, as the following selections reveal.

An Account of Captured Black Troops[1]

The Confederate Congress had enacted that negro troops, captured, should be restored to their owners. We had several hundreds of such, taken by Forrest in Tennessee, whose owners could not be reached; and they were put to work on the fortifications at Mobile, rather for the purpose of giving them healthy employment than for the value of the work. I made it a point to visit their camps and inspect the quantity and quality of their food, always found to be satisfactory. On one occasion, while so engaged, a fine-looking negro, who seemed to be leader among his comrades, approached me and said: "Thank you, Massa General, they give us plenty of good vituals; but how you like our work?" I replied that they had worked very well. "If you would give us guns we will fight for these works, too. We would rather fight for our own white folks than for strangers." And, doubtless, this was true. In their dealings with the negro the white men of the South should ever remember that no instance of outrage occurred during the war. Their wives and little ones remained safe at home, surrounded by thousands of faithful slaves, who worked quietly in the fields until removed by the Federals. This is the highest testimony to the kindness of the master and the gentleness of the servant; and all the dramatic talent prostituted to the dissemination of falsehood in "Uncle Tom's Cabin" and similar productions can not rebut it.

---

[1]From Richard Taylor, *Destruction and Reconstruction: Personal Experiences of the Late War* (New York, 1879).

"Colored Troops Fought Nobly"[2]

Mr. J. B. Briggs of Briggsville, Ky. (Muhlenberg County), says the *Louisville Times*, is the only person who commanded colored troops in action on the Confederate side during the war.

Mr. Briggs was Captain and Assistant Quartermaster of the Fourth Regiment Tennessee Volunteer Cavalry, C.S.A. and served during the war with Wheeler and Forrest. . . . The Fourth Tennessee thus secured a full share of these recruits and was always comparatively full.

At the battle of Chickamauga the Fourth Tennessee Cavalry was dismounted to fight as infantry, every fourth man being told off to hold horses. These horse-holders, and also all of the colored servants, were kept in the rear. The colored men numbered about 40, and having been in service a long time, had gradually armed themselves. Some of them were even better equipped than their masters, for on successful raids and battles they could follow in the rear and pick up those things that the soldiers had no time to secure; so that these colored servants could each boast of one or two revolvers and a fine carbine or repeating rifle.

During all of the early part of the battle of Chickamauga, the Fourth Tennessee Cavalry had been fighting as infantry, and as it became evident that a victory was to be won, Col. McLemore, commanding, ordered Captain Briggs to return to the horse-holders, and after placing the horses, teams, etc., under charge of the servants, to bring up the quarter of the regiment in charge of the horses so that they might take part in the final triumph. Capt. Briggs, on reaching the horses, was surprised to find the colored men organized and equipped, under Daniel McLemore, colored (servant to the Colonel of the regiment), and demanding the right to go into the fight. After trying to dissuade them from this, Capt. Briggs led them up to the line of battle which was just then preparing to assault Gen. Thomas's position. Thinking they would be of service in caring for the wounded, Capt. Briggs held them close up the line, but when the advance was ordered the negro company became enthused as well as their masters, and filled a portion of the line of advance as well as any company of the regiment.

---

[2] From the *Hawkinsville* (Ga.) *Dispatch*, Feb. 5, 1885.

While they had no guidon or muster roll, the burial after the battle of four of their number and the care of seven wounded at the hospital, told the tale of how well they fought that day.

"Anecdotes of Some of Those who Went Out in '61 with Their 'Young Marsters' of Company D"[3]

I will, as I promised in my last article, try to tell in a disconnected way something of the faithfulness and loyalty of the Southern slaves during the Civil war.

They all knew that the Northern army was fighting for their freedom, and that the Southern army was fighting to keep them in slavery. Strange as it may appear, they were as attentive, and worked as hard for their owners, with a few exceptions--as they ever had, and freely given up their sons to go to the war with their "young marsters," as body servants knowing that they would share alike the hardships and dangers of war.

I will right here relate a little incident showing how devoted they were to their owners. It was customary for the negroes on a plantation to meet at a cabin and have religious services. The "overseer" or "agent" as they are called now would usually go out and watch to see if nothing wrong was carried on. On one occasion my mother was left alone on the plantation and hearing them at a late hour singing and praying more fervently than usual went out and quietly looked on from an outside corner of the chimney. One of the young negro men was down on his knees praying for the safety and protection of his young master in the war (who was none other than myself,) and for his speedy return. My mother said she was so completely overcome at the fervency of his prayer that she knelt and joined him. She left quietly, and none of the negroes knew that she had ever been near them.

Those who went to the army to wait on their young masters seemed to anticipate their every want. They would go out "foraging" and get up everything they could to cook; carry their masters knap sack and guard his effects, which consisted of a little writing material, a Bible, his sweethearts picture and letters, and a very few clothes.

---

[3]By Capt. J. W. Williams, Co. D, 5th Ala. Inf. from an article which appeared in the *Greensboro* (Ala.) *Record*, Oct. 22, 1903.

How many times have we been out on the firing line, and after midnight perhaps tramping through sleet and snow, would we see twenty or thirty of these faithful negroes come up with their masters rations cooked for him.

They knew to what command their masters belonged, and would continue to inquire until they would find the right one. To the credit of the Confederate soldier I will say that I never knew one to try to take the rations away from one of the negroes, and on the other hand I never knew a negro to sell the rations, although they could have gotten almost their own price. They never seemed so happy as when they could get up something extra for their "young marster."

They knew the position of both armies as well as we did, and at any hour could have crossed over into the Yankee lines and been free. But out of the thousands, I knew of but very few that ever took advantage of this. Nearly all came back after the war, or if their owner died or was killed they would bring his body home, or see that he was buried and bring his effects home to his family.

Their devotion to their masters when they were sick or wounded was beautiful. I had occasion after the seven days fight around Richmond to go to the city to look up the wounded men of Co. "D," of which they were about forty. The Chimbora[z]o was the largest Hospital in Richmond, having about thirty wards, and each ward being about twice as large as any church in Greensboro, and built "box style." I went to the head surgeon to see if any of my company was there. I gave him the Masonic sign, which I always did when I wanted a favor. He recognized it and called his clerk and told him to take me through the hospital and see if I could find any of my company as they had been too busy to make out a roll of the wounded. We passed through ward after ward and in every one sat two or three of those kind sympathetic, black faces, watching over and caring for every want of their young masters. I then passed on into what they called the deadhouse. I think there was thirty or forty poor soldiers lying there cold and stiff in death. In there was one of those faithful negroes sitting by his dead master, waiting and watching for a wagon to come to take him to his last resting place; he being the only follower to the grave. After shedding a few tears perhaps he returned to the hospital, gathered up the blood stained clothes to carry home to "old Miss." He had done what he could. All honor these faithful souls and I believe they will have their reward.

Lieutenant Alfred Moore was killed at Chicka[hominy]. Pleas, his body servant went after dark to the Regiment and learned that his young master [was] dead, and between the two lines of battle. Pleas slipped in, found the body, placed it on a horse in front of him, and carried him to the nearest station, made a coffin and brought him home to his family. Lieut. Jim Hutchinson was killed at Spottsylvania Court House. When his father came for his remains he found they were inside the Federal lines. He took George (Lieut. Hutchinson's servant) and went in after the body. While they were inside the lines the Yankees tried to persuade George to stay with them and be a free man; threatened him in every way, but George was firm as a rock and came back to Greensboro, where he lived and died.

One of our company, whose name I will not give, but who was one of the best and most conscientious soldiers and gentlemen that ever lived, thought it was his duty to look after the spiritual welfare of his servant. On one occasion just on the eve of battle he carried his negro, who was a fat, sleek, good natured, sleepy-headed fellow, into the woods to read the Bible and pray with him. While he was in the midst [of] his devotions, he glanced at the negro and found to his surprise and mortification that he was fast asleep. The soldier walked back quietly, got him a brush and came down on the negroes head with the exclamation "you d _ _ _ rascal, how dare you treat me with such disrespect when I am looking after the welfare of your soul?" I have often heard them both laugh about it.

Jack Wynn, one of Co. "D," had a servant named Carey; a little black good natured negro, who could show more of his teeth and whites of eyes than anyone I ever saw. When we passed through Montgomery on our way to the army a good many of the soldiers passed in front of a drug store where there was sign of a full sized black negro with a mortar. Carey never forgetting his politeness, raised his hat and made a most profound bow. Of course the bow was not returned. The soldiers urged him to try it again with the same result. Carey felt insulted, and said: "Nigger you haint washed your face in a year, Look at the cob-webs in your har, I wouldn't be so consaited."

When the army was advancing the negro servants would always march by the side of their companies and would laugh and talk with the soldiers. They would sit around the camp fires with their masters ready at any time to do their bidding. The soldiers were always ready to help them in any way. I never saw but one whipped during the war. Co "D" had I expect as many as 30 negroes, first and last, and every one came home with their masters, except one belonging to Wiley Tunstall. Sandy came up to "Mars Wiley" and asked him for some money to go out foraging and he was never heard from afterwards; suppose he went to the Yankees.

Out of the number of negroes that went with Co. "D" only three are now living. We all feel attached to them, and never pass one of them without giving them a hearty handshake. In my opinion, in erecting monuments to the Confederate dead, it would be nothing but just and right to have a block of marble to commemorate the faithfulness of these people.

A Tribute to "Uncle" Jerry Perkins[4]

Charles Perkins enlisted at Brownsville, Tenn., under Capt. H. S. Bradford, who was afterwards Col. Bradford, of the 31st Tennessee Infantry. He was killed in the battle near Atlanta July 22, 1864. The boy Jerry went with him as a body servant. Before leaving, Charley's mother told Jerry that he must bring his "Marse Charley" back to her, and he promised that he would do it; that he would take him back alive or dead.

On that fateful July 22 young Perkins was killed; and when the regiment fell back to bivouac for the night, Jerry was alarmed not to see Marse Charley, and, upon being told that he was dead, said, "Here's your supper. I'm going to find Marse Charley," and away in the darkness he went. In a short while he returned, carrying the dead body of his young master on his back. He carried it a mile or so farther to a farmhouse, got some plank, borrowed a saw, hatchet, and nails, made a box, dug a grave, and buried him in the farmer's yard. He walked from Atlanta to Brownsville, Tenn., and reported the sad news. He was supplied with a farm wagon and a metallic

---

[4]Submitted by J. W. McClish of Brownsville, Tenn., and published in the *Confederate Veteran* 13 (1905).

coffin, went back to Georgia, disinterred the body of Charley Perkins, and hauled it home to Brownsville.

"Tribute to Aleck Kean in Virginia"[5]

Early in November, 1911, three of us, ex-members of the second company of Richmond Howitzers during the war of the sixties, honored ourselves by attending the funeral services of Alex Kean, which took place near Green Springs, in Louisa County. The career of Aleck as an honest, upright, faithful servant and man was so conspicuous and unique that it deserves this public notice.

When the war broke out, John Henry Vest, a son of the late James M. Vest, of Louisa, entered the Confederate army as a private in the second company of Richmond Howitzers, and took Aleck along as his body servant and cook, as was customary in those days. The "Renfrew" mess was soon formed with Aleck as the cook, and without hesitation I affirm that he was the most faithful and efficient man in the performance of every duty pertaining to his sphere that I have ever known. His whole mind and soul seemed bent on trying to get and prepare something for his mess to eat; and if there was anything to be gotten honestly, Aleck always got the share which was coming to his mess, and he always had that share prepared in the shortest time possible and in the most delicious way in which it could have been prepared in camp. The comfort of having such a man as Aleck around us in those trying times can scarcely be described and certainly cannot be exaggerated.

Young Mr. Vest (Aleck's young master) died in the fall of 1863, and after that Aleck, although he had offers to go to others or to return to his home, had become so attached to the members of the "Renfrew" mess that he refused to leave them, and, with his master's consent, remained with that mess up to the very last, when he surrendered with them near Appomattox. He was always loyal, true, brave, honest, and faithful not only to the members of his mess but to every man in the 2d and 3d Howitzers, all of whom knew, respected, and admired his fidelity and efficiency.

---

[5]Contributed by Judge George L. Christian of Richmond, Va., and published in the *Confederate Veteran* 20 (1912).

JERRY PERKINS

.... His funeral was largely attended both by white and colored, all of whom seemed anxious to attest by their presence the high regard in which he was held both as a man and a Christian....

"Gratitude of a Faithful Servant"[6]

I thank you for putting my picture in your magazine. I am proud of my war record. I was given when a young man by my old master, Samuel C. Williams, who was a member of the Virginia Secession Convention, to his oldest son, who was then Lieut. James H. Williams, of Chew's Battery, and I stood by him and his brothers until the close of the war. I was taken prisoner twice, captured once with the watches and money of our boys and others of the Williams mess upon my person, given into my care when the battle began. I escaped and returned with watches and money all safe.

The picture you published was taken while Dr. Averitt was on a visit to Mrs. James H. Williams at Woodstock, Va. I was not Dr. Averitt's camp servant, nor was he ever a member of the Williams mess. As far as I know, Dr. William McGuire, of Winchester, Va., L. B. Morel of Florida, and myself are the only living members of that mess. Rev. Dr. Averitt was often our guest.

Like the rest of the veterans, I am growing old; but I am with my people in Woodstock, where I was born.

The Gallantry of Georgia Slaves at the Front[7]

Captain R. B. Nisbet of Eatonton, when leaving for Norfolk with the "Brown Rifles," took with him as a body servant Dave, a son of "Old Austin," so well known to our citizens, as an old and faithful family servant of Judge Nisbet.

---

[6] From a letter written by "Black Hawk" of Woodstock, Va., and published in the *Confederate Veteran* 20 (1912).

[7] The following two accounts are drawn from a series of typescripted letters, narratives, and statements collected in the 1930s by the Georgia Division of the United Daughters of the Confederacy, known as "Reminiscences of Confederate Soldiers, 1861-1865," located in the Georgia Department of Archives and History, Atlanta.

Dave, on his arrival at Norfolk, was duly installed as cook for his master, but having an eye to business, it was not long before he had established an Ice Cream Saloon, having employed a colored female cook to perform his culinary duties, permission was granted, of course.

When the expedition to Chicomicomico was undertaken, Dave gallantly accompanied his master, equipped with musket, cartridge box etc. Notwithstanding the rapidity with which our boys pursued the fleet footed Hessians, he maintained his position in the very front ranks, until Col. Wright's horse was shot, at which time he was the only Confederate near the Colonel. But the rest of the story had better be told in the words of Davy himself, who is now at home on a visit to his family.

Says he, in narrating the incident, which he does with great gusto: "I was de only one near Mars. Wright at de time, and when de Yankee fired, de Colonel's horse fell and he pitched over his neck. One Yankee raised his gun and took aim at de Colonel, who said to me 'Davy are you charged?' "Yes, Colonel, I replied." 'Then shoot them Yankees.' I brought my gun to my shoulder [says Davy, suiting the action to the word] when de Yankee laid down his gun and said 'I surrender.' Mars. Wright he jumps up and says 'You are my prisoners.' They all replied 'We surrender, we are your prisoners.' Says Mars. Wright to me, 'Davy, take those men and march em off.' Says I 'Gentlemen, fall into line,' and dey fell into line, and I marched 'em off to do camp."

The above narration is true and exhibits the spirit that animates the intelligent portion of our slave population.

* * *

Reuben Weston Cleveland born March 14, 1843. I left Elberton with the first volunteers from the county. I was in Lynchburg, Va. when the first battle of Manassas was fought.

I was a participant in the second battle of Manassas. I was first wounded in the battle at Sharpsburg M.D., being shot through the left lung. My shoulder blade was shattered, so I came home on furlough. The hole was left open for seven months so the pus could drain out. Finally I got well and to my Company, I 15 Ga. Volunteers.

I was next wounded at the battle of Gettysburg, a bad flesh wound on the knee. I was squatting and the yankee that shot me was within ten feet of me. I managed to get home again by the help of a negro servant, who was captured three times by the enemy but always managed to get away and come back to me. I got well again and went back to my company. A ball cut a groove along my skull, at the battle of the Wilderness. I was sent to Lynchburg, Va. to a hospital where I had a bad time but being a man of tremendous constitution I got well again. I was never sick except a spell of measles. I was in active duty till Lee surrendered at Appomattox, Va. I was in many skirmishes not mentioned here. I was Top Sergeant at the time of the surrender. After being paroled I walked home, arriving there on the 29th day of April.

I am now 91 years old and nearly six months. I am living at Elberton, Georgia.

A Confederate Artilleryman Remembered[8]

Lewis Lejay, or Legree, whom I called "Daddy Lewis," a black man, was probably the only black or white Legree who lived in the Red River Valley. The son of Nanny House, Lewis was born in 1837 at Land's End, on the plantation of Col. Henry Marshall in northwest Louisiana. Marshall was a large cotton planter, owning by 1860 eight thousand acres and more than two hundred slaves. He later served in the Confederate Congress.

I got to know Daddy Lewis in 1917, when my father [Dr. Francis Scrimzeour Furman] went into the army and we rented our home and moved for a few months to live with my aunt, who lived at Land's End. After graduating from the First School of Gas Warfare at Fort Sill, Oklahoma, my father stayed with us for a few days before reporting as Chief of Gas Defense at Camp Beauregard, Louisiana. He arrived on a night train, and we met him and rode in a buggy seven miles to my aunt's place. Early the next morning, Lewis was there. Father spent most of the day with the old man, and I tagged along. Daddy Lewis gave my father some advice, particularly what to do if he ever got into action, became frightened, and how to act.

---

[8]Contributed by Francis Chandler Furman of Rolla, Missouri, as related in 1970 by his father, Greene Chandler Furman.

At my age of twelve, the idea of my father being scared of anything seemed incredible to me. Moreover, I doubted what Lewis could know about war. Father said: "Well, sometime you get him to talk. He'll probably talk more freely to you than anybody, but he knew a great deal about war and, in fact, was wounded in battle."

After Father had left for camp, Lewis came to the house several times, and I began to ask the old man about his experiences. In substance, his story is as follows:

"Along about the second year of the War old Marse Henry [Marshall] sent a bunch of wagons and drivers down to serve with the Army then in South Louisiana. I and several other men and wagons were attached to the Pelican Battery of Frenchmans from New Orleans. [The Pelican Battery was sworn into service at Napoleonville after the fall of New Orleans.] A lot of their women and children had left the City with them and they were living in the country district around, often without a roof or proper cover. A Captain [T. A.] Faries commanded the Battery" [5th Field Battery, Pelican Light Artillery].

"At the time they were down near Berwick Bay or Bayou Tech; a boat called the *Cotton Blossom* [*J. A. Cotton,* a 549-ton, partial-ironclad, side-wheel, gunboat, with a bow 32-pounder and an aft 9-pounder, commanded by Capt. Edward W. Fuller] was on a sandbar where they were using a lot of railroad iron to try and make an ironclad out of her. The Pelican Battery and some other troops were guarding the works as we knew Yankees were around. Just before Christmas Captain Faries came to me and talked around and about for some time about how a lot of men had to get off for Christmas and go see their folks and do what they could for them, and the Captain himself was going to take off for a few days. He said, 'Lewis, you know that'll make us mighty shorthanded.' I said, 'Yes, Sir.' He says, 'You know it's against the law for you to fight.' I said, 'Yes, Sir, but I don't mind.' He said, 'Well, remember I'm not asking you to fight but if the Yankees attacked us do you think you could help with the guns?' I said, 'Yes, Sir, I'll do it, you ain't asked be to do it but I'll do it.' Well, the Captain pondered a bit and then said, 'Do you think you can take No. four man on No. 2 Gun?' I said, 'Yes, Sir.' 'Well, I'll be much relieved to know you're there if any trouble comes up.' And I began to study what No. 4 did."

"When the gun was wired No. 4 had a bucket and water and a sponge was put in the water and some sloshed down the barrel and then I'd help the No. 2 swab out the gun. We had to do this because our powder was in cotton bagging and the embers left in the gun might set the powder off and blow the shoulders off the men with the rammer staff. The Yankees didn't have to be so careful because they had silk bagging for their powder and there weren't many embers left. Therefore they could fire faster then we could. After the barrel was swabbed out the No. 4 would put the bag of powder in and help the No. 2 ram it down the barrel. In the meantime, No. 3 covered the touch hole with a pad to keep air out, so if any embers were left it would not explode so easily. The No. 1 and the gunner would lay the piece and it would be rolled back in position and ready to fire--just like loading an old, muzzle-loading shotgun. Two of our guns were placed in brush along the sandbar. The other two guns were put back in the rear. My gun was on the sandbar."

"Right after Christmas [probably on December 31, 1862, and possibly again on New Year's Day, 1863] the Yankees came up to get the *Cotton Blossom*. We knew they were coming, and the orders were to load with grapeshot or canister. We didn't have either grapeshot or canister but we put in a bag of rock and small pieces of iron, had our extra loads arranged and waited for the Yankees to come. By-and-by they came up and we had a skirmish line to shoot with then a while and some shots were fired from the *Cotton Blossom*, but the men on the *Cotton Blossom* were told to leave and they started running away. The Yankees, seeing this, came awhoopin' and ahollerin'--not like our boys, but a sort of chantin' like they did--and when their line was parallel with ours our two guns opened--keblam--and the other two guns began to fire shell toward their rear position."

I asked Lewis, "Did that end the fighting?" He said, "Yes, Sir. They never came back, even to pick up their wounded. We'uns always did if it was at all possible, but they didn't seem to care for their own people. After that, the *Cotton Blossom* was taken off the sandbar and moved up the bayou."

"A few months after this [February 1863] our wagons were sent to help build Fort Debussy, on the Red River, in Avoielles Parish below Alexandria. We were proceeding along the road alongside a little bayou when the Yankees opened up an ambush from across a little bayou. One of my mules was shot and killed and I got out to cut him loose and was fixing up the harness when a bullet in the shoulder knocked me down." [Lewis still carried the bullet and, no doubt sensing that I didn't believe him, allowed me to feel it.]

At about this time the panic started. According to Lewis, the white wagonmaster was the first to start running away. "Preacher Bob Sloan went by, in a hurry, shoutin' 'My God! They done killed Lewis,' and I guess I was pretty bloody. Pomp Ferguson, who belonged to your Uncle John, also went by in a hurry, but the wagonmaster, who was on horseback, led all the rest. However, when things quieted down I got up and led my remainin' mule and wagon into the bushes and the Yankees did not pursue us. After a while I rearranged the wagonload, puttin' a lot of junk on top, with the powder for the Battery on the bottom, and after dark drove on through to where we were. I could hardly lift my arm, and when I rejoined the outfit the old Captain said he was sure glad to see me because we needed that powder and they had all figured I was dead."

I asked Daddy Lewis if the Yankees had seen him as he got away. He said, "Yes, their pickets stopped me in the middle of the night but I told 'em I was just a nigger refugeein' and they looked at the junk on the top of the wagon and let me get by." I asked him what they would have done if they had known about the powder in the bottom. "Oh," he said, "I guess they would have hung me--if they'd had time. They did not like colored people standing by their own white folks, as most of us did. I was not the only one shot that day; Daniel Bogan from the River Place died of wounds received then."

After the war, Daddy Lewis bought some sixty acres of land from my grandmother and lived on it until he died, November 3, 1921. In an old record book my father wrote: "Lewis Legree, son of Nanny H born 1837 Died Nov. 3, 1921 a faithful and devoted servant. He served as waggoner in the Confederate Army and was slightly wounded in escaping with his wagon thru the Federal lines."

Daddy Lewis Legree and Capt. Francis Scrimzeour Furman in the summer of 1917, at the well behind Land's End Plantation, Desoto Parish, La.
Courtesy Francis Chandler Furman

Joseph T. Wilson, *The Black Phalanx; A History of The Negro Soldiers of The United States* (1890)

This remarkable book was written by a veteran of the 2nd Louisiana Native Guards and of the 54th Massachusetts Regiment, whose saga was vividly portrayed in the Hollywood motion picture Glory. *After the war Wilson, a noted speaker, was active in the Grand Army of the Republic, a national organization of Union veterans. The excerpt reprinted below is from Wilson's chapter entitled "The Confederate Service," in which the author deals with the question of what motivated blacks to fight for the Confederacy.*

The leaders at the South in preparing for hostilities showed the people of the North, and the authorities at Washington, that they intended to carry on the war with no want of spirit; that every energy, every nerve, was to be taxed to its utmost tension, and that not only every white man, but, if necessary, every black man should be made to contribute to the success of the cause for which the war was inaugurated. Consequently, with the enrollment of the whites began the employment of the blacks. . . .

. . . . [In] April, 1861, the free negroes of New Orleans, La., held a public meeting and began the organization of a battalion, with officers of their own race, with the approval of the *State* government, which commissioned their negro officers. When the Louisiana militia was reviewed, the Native Guards (negro) made up, in part, the first division of the State troops. . . .

[*Wilson notes how in antebellum New Orleans the population of "colored people" was of diverse ethnicity: English, French, Portuguese, Spanish, African, and West Indian.*]

It was from these classes that the 1,400 colored men, forming the Native Guard regiment, came, and which recruited to 3,000 before the city was captured by the Union fleet. This brigade was placed at the United States Mint building, under command of a creole, who, instead of following the confederate troops out of the city when they evacuated it, allowed his command to be cut off, and surrendered to General Butler.

Of course, prior to this date, the negro at the South had taken an active part in the preparations for war, building breastworks, mounting cannon, digging rifle-pits and entrenchments, to shield and protect his rebelling master. . . .

[*Wilson quotes from a telegram from South Carolina and a report from the* Charleston Mercury, *which indicated early in the war that blacks were involved in erecting defense works. He also cited part of the Tennessee law of June 1861, which authorized the recruitment of "all male free persons of color, between the ages of 15 and 50."*]

A few months after, the Memphis *Avalanche*, of September 3rd, 1861, exultingly announced the appearance on the streets of Memphis, of two regiments of negroes, under command of confederate officers. . . .

Nor were the negroes in Virginia behind those of the other Southern States. In April, the Lynchburg *Republican* chronicled the enrollment of a company of free negroes in that city, also one in Petersburg.

Thus instead of revolts among the negroes, slaves and free, as predicted by some Union men at the North, many became possessed of a fervor,--originating generally in fear,--stimulated by an enthusiasm of the whites, that swept the populace like a mighty sea current into the channel of war. The negro who boasted the loudest of his desire to fight the Yankees; who showed the greatest anxiety to aid the confederates, was granted the most freedom and received the approval of his master.

. . . . There was also an intuitive force that led them, and they unhestitatingly followed, feeling that though they took up arms against the National Government, freedom was the ultimatum. Many of those who enlisted feared to do otherwise than fight for slavery, for to refuse would have invited, perchance, torture if not massacre; to avert which many of the free blacks, as well as some of the slaves, gave an apparent acquiescence to the fervor of their lesser informed comrades, who regarded any remove from the monotony of plantation life a respite.

The readiness with which they responded to the call was only astonishing to those who were unacquainted with the true feelings of the unhappy race whose highest hope of freedom was beyond the pearly gates of the celestial domain. One thing that impressed the blacks greatly was the failure of Denmark Vesy, Nat Turner and John Brown, whose fate was ever held up to them as the fate of all who attempted to free themselves or the slaves. Escape to free land was the only possible relief they saw on earth, and *that* they realized as an individual venture, far removed from the field-hand South of Delaware, Maryland and Virginia.

It was not unnatural, then, for some to spring at the opportunity offered to dig trenches and assist Beauregard in mounting cannon, and loading them with shot and shell to fire upon Fort Sumter.

The negro did not at first realize a fight of any magnitude possible, or that it would result in any possible good to himself. So while the *free* negroes trembled because they *were* free, the slaves sought refuge from suspicion of wanting to be free, behind, *per se,* an enthusiasm springing, not from a desire and hope for the success of the confederates, but from a puerile ambition to enjoy the holiday excitement.

Later on, however, when the war opened in earnest, and the question of the freedom and slavery of the negro entered into the struggle; when extra care was taken to guide him to the rear at night; when after a few thousand Yankee prisoners, taken in battle, had sought and obtained an opportunity of whispering to him the *real* cause of the war, and the surety of the negroes' freedom if the North was victorious, the slave negro went to the breastworks with no less agility, but with prayers for the success of the Union troops, and a determination to go to the Yankees at the first opportunity; though he risked life in the undertaking. When the breastworks had been built and the heavy guns mounted, when a cordon of earth-works encircled the cities throughout the South, and after a few thousand negroes had made good their escape into the Union lines, then those who had labored upon the fortifications of the South were sent back to the cotton-fields and the plantations to till the soil to supply the needs of the confederate soldiers who were fighting to keep them in bondage. But when the policy of the North was changed and union and *liberty* were made the issues of the struggle, as against slavery and disunion, and the Union forces began to slay their enemies, the Confederate Government realized the necessity of calling the negroes from the hoe to the musket,--from the plantations to the battle-fields. . . .

Henry W. Thomas, *History of the Doles-Cook Brigade, Army of Northern Virginia* (1903)

A native of Eatonton, Georgia, Henry W. Thomas entered Confederate service on May 14, 1862, as a private in Company G, "Putnam Light Infantry," 12th Georgia Regiment, which was brigaded with the 4th, 21st, and 44th Georgia regiments to form the Doles-Cook Brigade. From the Seven Days campaign to Gettysburg, Cold Harbor, and Appomattox, the Doles-Cook Brigade was in the midst of the hottest action. It took terrific losses at Mechanicsville and at Malvern Hill, while its commanding general, George P. Doles of Milledgeville, was killed on June 2, 1864, at Bethesda Church. Although captured and exchanged early in the war, Private Thomas fought to the bitter end, witnessing the surrender of Lee's army at Appomattox. He was 22 years old. The following selection is from Thomas's chapter entitled "The Negro," which chronicles the exploits of a number of black servants who accompanied the brigade, including Thomas's own servant, Morris.

George Wallace served through the entire war as a body-servant of Captain Howard Tinsley, and was at the surrender of Lee's army. He rode General Cook's famous war-horse "Old Whitey" home and turned him over to Mr. Winship, a brother-in-law of the general, as he was still in prison. . . .

George became a politician and was elected to the State Senate during the Bullock regime. He now holds a position in the post office in Macon, Ga.

"Pete" was the carriage-driver of Colonel Tim M. Furlow, of Americus. "Pete" went to the war with his young master, the gallant William L. Furlow, captain of Company D, Twelfth Georgia Regiment. Captain Dawson was captain of Company A and W. H. Turpin was first lieutenant. These officers were under "Stonewall" Jackson. In the battle at McDowell, Va., on the 8th of May, 1862, these three gallant and brave officers fell. Distance from the rail-

HENRY W. THOMAS
From The History of the Doles-Cook Brigade

roads, difficulty of transportation, decided those in authority to bury the three Georgians in Virginia's soil. But Pete, fond of the folks at home and devoted to his young master, would not consent. So persistent was he that the colonel of the Twelfth Georgia finally agreed to help the negro. They aided him in getting coffins for the three; and Pete, having the money of Captain Furlow, hired an ox-cart and hauled the bodies sixty miles to a railroad station; and, suffering delays, by sheer persistence got the remains on the cars and finally brought them to Americus. . . .

Ab Lee went to Virginia with Lieutenant, afterwards Captain, A. S. Reid, of the Twelfth Georgia Regiment, as his body-servant, and remained with him until the surrender. He was an honorary member of the Confederate Veterans' Association of Putnam County, and also of the Doles-Cook Brigade Survivors' Association. He is now living in his old home at Eatonton, Ga.

Dick, the body-servant of R. H. and W. F. Jenkins, Company G, Twelfth Georgia Regiment, was a good-hearted and handy man, always in good humor and very obedient. At the battle of Chancellorsville, on Sunday morning after the Yankees had been driven some distance, Dick went on the battle-field to rob dead Yankees. He soon came upon one with an elegant pair of boots, which he concluded to appropriate to his own use. He took hold of his foot and commenced to pull at the boot, but the supposed dead man spoke in a feeble voice and asked him to please give him a little water. This speech so frightened Dick that, instead of complying with the dying man's request, he fled precipitately.

Isham, commonly called "Smut" because he was so black, was the body-servant of Lieutenant Stephen B. Marshall, of the Putnam Light Infantry, Company G, Twelfth Georgia Regiment. He was the liveliest and rarest darkey in the regiment. Always in trouble but never out of humor, every one picked at him and had some joke to tell on him. . . .

At the battle of Alleghany Mountain a shell exploded near Isham, when he immediately mounted a bare-back mule, his face toward the tail of the beast, and the mule was rapidly driven to the rear by the use of Isham's heels and pole; both the mule and negro were missing for two or three days. When he returned Marshall asked him why he left, when he promptly answered: ["]Because 'a good run is better than a bad stand,' for had I remained and received a wound or been killed, I could not have served you as I promised old master I would."

Isham went to his reward several years ago, and it is hoped that he reached a better and happier home beyond the skies.

Morris, the body-servant of H. W. Thomas of the Putnam Light Infantry, Company G, Twelfth Georgia Regiment, was a good, true and faithful man, ever ready to perform any and all duties required of him. He never crossed the Potomac; would always get permission to remain in Virginia when our army invaded Maryland and Pennsylvania for fear of being captured, but came promptly to camp and reported for duty as soon as the army returned to Virginia. Whenever bullets commenced to fly and shells to whistle he invariably sought the rear. When asked why he did not remain with or near his white friends who had to face the enemy, he would reply, "You are white and I am a negro and can't stand the racket." He was at the surrender and walked every step of the way home with his master, and remained with him until advised to hunt a job and look out for himself. He was universally liked by the good people of Eatonton because he was polite, accommodating and knew his place. He died with consumption about eight years after the surrender, and the writer hopes that the change was a happy one.

William C. Oates, *"The Negro as Slaves and Soldiers" In the War Between the Union and the Confederacy and Its Lost Opportunities* (1904)

William Calvin Oates entered Confederate service with the 15th Alabama Infantry and rose to the rank of colonel under Gen. James Longstreet, Army of Northern Virginia. He commanded his unit in a number of battles, including Fredericksburg, Cedar Mountain, Chickamauga, and Gettysburg, where he reputedly observed Union wagon trains in the rear from his vantage point on Little Round Top. After the war Oates served as governor of Alabama, which he also represented in Congress. During the Spanish-American War he held the rank of brigadier general. In the following selection, Oates laments one particular "lost opportunity" of the Confederacy: its failure to utilize fully slaves as soldiers.

The greatest reason for military failures throughout the history of the world has been indecision as to what should be done, and when a decision was reached, tardiness in its execution. In great exigencies the same may be said of legislation; the Confederate Congress had ample time to consider, but could not see that opportunity until too late, and then saw it with but one eye.

President Davis, with a military education, was hesitant--loth to admit the necessity for the enlistment of negro soldiers. The Congress of Bourbon incapables, who could never see the length of their noses into the future, did nothing but register as laws the requests of Mr. Davis, and never perceived the necessity until General Lee and Davis said so. Lee never would give his opinion or advice until Davis as President called for it, and he was unreasonably hesitant. . . .

At last President Davis told the Congress to pass a law to enlist negro slaves as soldiers, and they did it, after months of wrangling--such a thing as it was. . . .

[*Here, Oates includes a reprint of the March 1865 act "to Increase the Military Force of the Confederate States," authorizing the President "to accept from the owners of slaves, the service of such number of able-bodied negro men as he may deem expedient, for and during the war, to perform military service in whatever capacity he may direct." The fifth and final section of the act read: "That nothing in this act shall be construed to authorize a change in the relation which the said slaves shall bear toward their owners, except by consent of the owners of the State in which they may reside, and in pursuance of the laws thereof."*]

The fifth section nullified the efficiency of the act. After providing them to volunteer and be organized into companies, regiments, brigades, etc., and to receive rations, clothing, and pay, the President to appoint the officers, comes section five, which says (nothwithstanding they may make good soldiers and fight hard to establish the independence of the Confederacy) that they should be and remain slaves, unless the owner saw proper to set them free. A negro who did not have sense enough, under that law, to have deserted to the enemy at the first opportunity would have been too much of an idiot to have made a soldier. No sensible negro would have volunteered under that law, if honestly explained to him, unless it was for the purpose of availing himself of the opportunity it would have given him to desert to the other side, where he could, beyond doubt, have obtained his freedom. He would have done this rather than fight, with chances of being killed, or of having his body mangled with shot and shell to keep himself and his children after him in slavery. . . .

The only defense possible for that section is to claim that the Congress did not have the constitutional power to strike down or annul any one's property in his slave. That was a weakling's excuse. In such an exigency as the Confederacy was then in, a man's property in the slave should have been consficated. The title of the owner was so jeopardized that it was practically worthless. That was an instance wherein necessity should alone have governed the action of the Confederate Congress. Whenever an act becomes necessary to preserve the existence of the government itself, the Constitution is no restraint. It was so regarded in the passage of the Conscript act. Being into the war, the Confederates should have used every honorable means to have attained success.

Notwithstanding the defects in the law, a few companies were raised under it in Virginia, the owners giving the slaves their freedom. Soon after the law was passed the Secretary of War and Adjutant-General went actively to work to put it into operation. General Lee issued an order for that purpose. General Johnston, then commanding in North Carolina, under orders from the War Department, detailed Brig.-Gen. John T. Morgan (now the senior United States Senator from Alabama) to come to Alabama and superintend the enlistment of negroes within the State. Capt. Wm. B. Jones, of the Third Alabama Regiment (now a prominent citizen of Montgomery, Alabama), and other company officers, came home to aid in the work and obtain commands. But before General Morgan got his work under way Appomattox was reached, and Lee's surrender put an end to all enlistments.

[*Oates then speculates what impact the enlistment of 300,000 black soldiers in the Confederate armies would have made at the time, and earlier in the war.*]

. . . . If at Gettysburg Lee had had 50,000 negro troops under white officers, as additional force, he would have walked all over Meade's army, have gone to Philadelphia and peace would then have been made. . . .

Among the Confederate generals of distinction who favored the enlistment of the negroes in the Confederate armies, were Ewell, Johnston, Hood, Cleburne, Gordon, Hill, R. E. Lee, and others.

By the failure of the Confederate Congress to realize the vast importance of timely action to offset or nullify the act of Lincoln in issuing the emancipation proclamation, one of the greatest opportunities the Confederates ever had for realization was lost forever. . . .

A History of Lumsden's Battery, C.S.A. (1905)

Commanded by Capt. Charles L. Lumsden, Lumsden's battery was composed of men from the Tuscaloosa, Alabama, area. This hard-fought unit participated with the Army of Tennessee in a number of major battles, including Perryville, Murfreesboro, Chickamauga, Chattanooga, Atlanta, and Nashville. In 1905 two former members of the unit, George Little and James R. Maxwell, wrote a short history of the battery. They also included several anecdotes about the dozen or so body servants who served primarily as company cooks. One cook in particular, Jim Bobbett, proved to be quite industrious, as the following selection reveals.

The negro slaves usually had money in their pockets, when their masters had none, that they made serving officers and men in many ways.

The writer's own servant, Jim Bobbett by name, had left his wife on my father's plantation in Tuscaloosa County, Alabama, but had no children. He was selected from several who desired the place, as being a handy fellow all round. A pure negro, with flat nose, and merry disposition. From mere love of myself and a determination to see that I should never lack food or clothing, as long as he could obtain the wherewithal to prevent it, he was faithful in the service of the government he was fighting for. He wore a broad flat waterproof belt next to his skin, and scarely ever had less than $100.00 therein, and often as high as $1,000.00. He was a good barber and clothes cleaner, and a handy man in many ways, and a few weeks stop of the army in camp soon replenished his "bank" and out of it he generally procured what was needed for me or himself or his friends, without any interference or direction from me.

If he got more than he needed, he disposed of his surplus at a profit. I suppose that if neither a slick tongue nor money would procure necessities, he did not hesitate to "press" them. But his jolly flattering tongue, with the women of his race, along our routes made him their favorite, and when he bade them "goodbye" his "grub" bucket would be filled with the best to be had. When he and his pals were behind, when the wagon train came up, we did not kick, but would turn in, perhaps supperless, to sleep, knowing that some time before day, they would arrive with something to fill us up. . . .

★ FACING THE REALITY OF SOUTHERN HISTORY ★

EDWARD C. RAFFETTO

> Much is said about the slaves coming into the Federal lines, and many complaints are made because they are not promptly given up. Are they not in the Confederate lines, and are they not used to build fortifications and do the work of rebels, and in many instances used to man rebel guns, and fight against the Union?
>
> *The Liberator*, July 18, 1862

EVEN HONORED SCHOLARS REGULARLY ENGAGE IN MAKING "history" into ideology. Ideology in this sense refers to a way of understanding reality which tries to bend reality in a certain direction. The key is the attempt to bend what is true. I think there is a genuine Truth we are able to reach, and that a right evaluation of reality illuminates it for us, leads us to it. But many in our world doubt there is any objective Truth or doubt the human capacity to reach it. They see it as their human work to try to invent their own "Truth" and engage in the scholarly bending of "facts" to achieve it. In terms of southern history, there is also the problem of proper theorization: how do we understand the material we find as it relates to African-Americans in Confederate service? Clearly the vast majority of blacks continued to work in the life circumstances they had. In what sense was this "black support for the Confederacy"? The Northern view is that they had no choice and waited for the chance to run to the U. S. army for freedom. We instinctively know that this cannot be a valid reading, even if for no other reason than this is not the way most people operate: they do not reduce themselves to the mere political and economic level. Life is bigger than that.

In 1972 two learned and distinguished scholars, Robert W. Fogel and Stanley Engerman, both certified liberals of impeccable credentials, produced a book entitled *Time On The Cross*. It was a study of actually measurable data on the life of slaves in the American South. It only looked at what we would call "historical facts," such as diet, clothing, housing and recorded treatment of those held in slavery. The authors clearly recognized the moral evil of slavery and had no intentions of doing anything which could be

---

The Reverend Raffetto is an Episcopal priest in Maryland, who for many years pastored a church with a biracial membership.

construed as supporting it. But they had to conclude that the life of the typical slave in the South was healthier, more pleasant and materially better than the life of the typical "free" laborer in the North. The clear majority of those who reviewed the book and of the whole scholarly community concluded that the authors were racists!

One has to understand the special definition of the word "racist" as some use it and the mood of the media (the powers which communicate between us in the wider society) in order to see how such an absurd conclusion could be widely accepted. It flies in the face of reason and is an utterly unfair accusation of two admirable and decent men. The argument against them seemed to be that, whatever the facts were, even mentioning them betrayed the present political struggle for African-American rights, as envisioned by the elite.

In 1989, Fogel published another book, *Without Consent Or Contract*, which attempted to show the nature of the institution of American slavery. In it he demonstrated the widespread racism of the North in the last century. Indeed, he presented conclusive evidence that the North won the great battle of the 1850s on the extension of slavery to the territories ("Bleeding Kansas") only by playing the so-called "race card": "We don't want blacks competing with white labor." "Keep the Territories white!"

Many scholars have noted the large number of abolitionists who were strongly racist. They opposed slavery from certain abstract political principles, not because they had a respect for the unique worth and dignity of every human being. Some of them hated the South because there were so many blacks there; they hated slavery because it kept the United States from being a "racially pure," white nation. Saying that American slavery was a morally evil institution does not necessarily mean that one also thinks that black people are worthy of respect.

Therefore, there is much historical evidence that supports conclusions which would surprize many thoughtful people in our nation today. The "peculiar institution" of the South (slavery) need not have been inherently racist and driven by racial hatred (many free blacks owned slaves); the "liberators" who opposed slavery could have been haters of black persons simply because they were black. In the South the personal contact of black and white persons, even under the constraints of institutional slavery, could have been more constructive, more real, more human, than was possible in the "free" North.

Consider this comparison. In a hundred years the vast majority of thoughtful, decent, and respectable persons may look upon the current system of government administered "welfare" programs, with their apparently correlated aspects of abuses, aimlessness, dependency and personal degradation, in much the same way that we look at slavery today. That is, they may evaluate our government "welfare" system just as we evaluate slavery: with condemnation and incomprehension. They may conclude, "It was an inhuman institution."

In our world one might well ask how any decent human being could think he or she held "title" to another human being like a piece of impersonal property. In a hundred years it is possible that a person in that world might ask how any decent human being could have tolerated--must less supported--a hugely destructive system of government administered "welfare."

In both cases one needs to remember that many decent, God-fearing people did. Some because (however mistakenly) they believed in "the system." Some because they could see no way out of it. Some because they did not think in abstract terms but knew that this particular man or woman was better off in practical terms with "the system" than without it.

One of my ancestors in Virginia, Jacob Weaver, died in 1821, and we have an accounting of his estate, which included a large number of slaves. The eldest Weaver children are recorded as assuming responsibility for the care of several aged slaves who were listed as having no monetary "value," but for whom Jacob Weaver had been responsible, by the law of God and of Virginia, to feed, clothe, house and care until they died. Slavery *is* evil, but it did have a human dimension missing from the Northern "free labor" system which cast people out without pity when they could no longer produce or were "no longer useful."

So, today, a person who positively hates the destruction which he believes the present government welfare system causes to its "beneficiaries" and to the whole community might nevertheless admit that in this case or that one, it has done some good. Certainly anyone must ask what will happen to its recipients and administrators if we abolish it.

Those who take for granted the evil of government welfare may condemn all who used or tolerated it as enslavers of their fellow human beings. Abstracted from reality, they may wax hot against the "haters" who allowed or exploited the system. But some who used or tolerated the system have a genuine respect for the personhood of the human beings caught in it, while some of those who today condemn the system may do so for very selfish and unjust motives. Will those who might condemn government welfare be able to distinguish between them? Perhaps this comparison may provide light to those today who so hotly condemn the southern experience and the Confederacy.

I am not arguing in defense of slavery or against government welfare. Still less am I suggesting that slavery was the central reason for secession (which seems to me to have been justified distrust of the winners of the 1860 election). I offer these general thoughts to illustrate the complexity of historical questions as they are actually lived. It is on the basis of this complexity that I assert that many Southerners were more constructively, humanly, in touch with the reality of black people and their personhood than many Yankees who shouted and marched for "freedom." In this aspect of the question abstract questions of political rights are relatively less important. Obviously they are vastly important, but they cannot embrace the totality of the human experience.

The difficulty many people have in accepting this concept is based, I think, on the widespread acceptance of the northern myth of the Civil War. It pervades the thinking of many in the media and in our schools. A myth is a story told to account for something. It does not need to be true, only to be accepted. A myth is used to support a popular enthusiasm, however dubious, such as "The United States exists first of all to exalt personal rights." The problem with myths is that, to the extent they are not actually true, they are deceptive and dangerous.

The distinguished southern writer, Robert Penn Warren, produced in 1958 a peaceful and broad-minded little book, *The Legacy of the Civil War: Meditations on the Centennial.* In it Warren gently speaks about the terrible costs of the War. Among them he includes the psychological cost of saddling the respective sections with myths. The South he describes as burdened with "The Great Alibi," which rendered it both guiltless and helpless. The North he describes as burdened with an unlovely psychological heritage he calls "The Treasury of Virtue," which asserts that the North is redeemed, justified, and exalted, by history (which Northerners, as victors, have rewritten to suit their own needs). They "know" that the War saved the Union and that slavery was the cause of the War. They have an image of Union power: "a boy in blue with one hand striking off iron shackles from a grizzle-headed Uncle Tom weeping in gratitude, and with the other passing out McGuffey's First Reader to a rolypoly pickaninny laughing in hope" (p. 60).

This northern myth now seems to be widespread throughout the United States as the American myth of the War; it certainly pervades the thinking of the elite. In this version of history the South seceded solely to preserve human chattel slavery, while the North smashed the South solely to establish human freedom (and the Union which supposedly guaranteed it). These simplistic notions are silly and indefensible but dominate and organize many peoples' thinking about the War, precisely because they are myths.

This generally accepted myth of the War tells us, as it is meant to, about ourselves, not about the events of one hundred and thirty years ago. Hence, anyone offering mere facts which suggest the myth is wrong, such as the nobility of honorable service to their country of Confederates, both black and white, is treading on dangerous ground. That interpretation threatens the very way some people understand themselves and their country. True to the abstractions that they love, the opponents of the Confederacy and of honoring black Southerners are not interested in what "really happened."

More than political argument is involved. Liberty is one of the great, formulative notions of the modern age. In one sense of the word, it was a dominant thought of our 1776 American revolution (and in the same sense of the word was dominant in the Confederate struggle for Independence.) Promoters of the myth of the Civil War delight in the first but cannot begin to grasp the second.

In the last three hundred and fifty years, personal and political freedoms have been watchwords zealously promoted by almost every interest. Even the Communists, of all people, used freedom as a slogan during their Russian coup in November 1917. Strangely, in terms of communist theory, it was perfectly reasonable for these murderous anti-human gangsters to do so. The word "freedom" must be defined, for it is something at the same time most deeply valued and most profoundly threatened.

For many, liberty (personal and political freedom) means being able to do what one wants to do when one wants to do it. This right enables me to be "who I am." For others, freedom means being able to live life in accordance with reality; that is, freedom to be qood. The first idea arises from what Dr. Thomas Sowell, a distinguished American scholar, has identified as the "unconstrained vision." Sowell's book on this subject, *Conflicts of Visions: Ideological Origins of Political Struggles* (1987), is of the greatest importance to understanding the political and social situation of our time.

Sowell sees differing visions, differing senses of how the world works, differing maps to travel by, as underlying much of the social and political struggle of the last 250 years. Today, there are two main, opposing, kinds of vision: the first he calls the "unconstrained;" the second he calls the "constrained." They differ not only in their understanding of how persons and societies work but also in their basic conceptions of the nature of man. "Those who see the potentialities of human nature as extending far beyond what is currently manifested have a social vision quite different from those who see human beings as tragically limited creatures," Sowell contends.

In the unconstrained vision the fundamental problem is not nature or man (which are good) but institutions; in the constrained vision institutions help restrain man's basic selfishness and destructiveness. In the first vision rules are degrading and unnecessary; in the second they are indispensable. In the first, good intentions and sincerity are centrally important; in the second, it is fidelity to the collective wisdom of the past which embodies the recognized benefits (mostly unintended) of all human activity. The first vision is convinced that foolish or immoral choices explain the evils of the world and that wiser and more humane social policies are the solution. The second vision sees evils as proceeding from limited and unhappy choices available, given the inherent moral and intellectual limitations of human beings. The first, therefore, relies on an intellectual and moral elite to dictate "solutions." The second relies on the common wisdom of everybody to find those social processes which allow the greatest good to flourish.

Perhaps most revealing is the unconstrained vision's insistence that, since everyone is so good, anyone who disagrees with the elite must do so because of gross immorality or madness. The constrained vision assumes that people make tragic mistakes. The unconstrained, therefore, find it very hard to admit that their "enemies" can be sincere or well-intentioned. The constrained vision has no trouble seeing those qualities in the other side, since sincerity and good intentions often accompany bad actions.

I have done little here but given a surface view of a profoundly well-reasoned book. Sowell does not deal with the War. Moreover, the two visions themselves arise in a secular world where God has been made "private," so neither vision could fully satisfy a believing Jew, Muslim, or Christian. Yet it helps explain a lot, such as why the different visions have different definitions of such basic ideas as power, justice, and equality.

What is going on in the attacks on the Confederacy, its people and its symbols? Why can any study of black support for the Confederacy can expect to be ignored or vehemently denounced? Sowell offers one perspective.

Mere reporting of historical facts is not enough. We must recognize the underlying visions which will deal with these in different ways. It is necessary for those with the unconstrained vision to reject the Confederacy and its symbols, and the noble part played in the struggle for independence by black Confederates. Thinking of such things suggest that their vision is defective. Further, the on-going struggle of these two visions has entered a heightened phase since the collapse of the Soviets. Those who believe in the unconstrained vision, though most opposed Communism as such, are feeling defensive. The widespread failure of the "solutions" proposed by those with an unconstrained vision leads those committed to this vision to more agitated, even desperate, defense of its assumed truth. In a sense they are defending what they consider to be their very selves.

The South and the Confederacy have long been targets for those with an unconstrained vision. Their explanation of the War in the northern myth requires all southern blacks to have supported the Union. To preserve the myth, it is necessary to abandon any thought of black Confederates.

Encountering the reality of southern history means that we must recognize the personage of all Confederates, both black and white, and come face to face with the complexity, glory, and tragedy of America's greatest war.

NEPTUNE SMALL OF ST. SIMONS ISLAND, GEORGIA
Courtesy Georgia Department of Archives and History

Born into slavery on September 15, 1831, Small went to war as a manservant to his master's son, Capt. Henry Lord King Page. Following the death of Captain King, Small ventured out under fire on the battlefield and retrieved his master's body and brought it to Savannah for burial at Christ Church. Afterward, Small returned to the warfront accompanying the youngest King son, Cuyler. After emancipation, Small was given a tract of land, where he built a small house and lived the remainder of his life. The house stood on property that is now known as Neptune Park.

NENE, WIFE OF CONFEDERATE MANSERVANT NEPTUNE SMALL
Courtesy Georgia Department of Archives and History

★ SOURCES FOR THE STUDY OF★ BLACK CONFEDERATES

GENE C. ARMISTEAD

ALTHOUGH THEIR NUMBERS WERE MANY AND THEIR SERVICES invaluable, little mention has been made of the black soldiers of the South in general literature. Nevertheless, innumerable references can be found in official records and correspondence, published works, newspaper articles, slave narratives, and veterans' accounts. The following will serve as a starting point for those interested in pursuing the subject for themselves.

PUBLISHED WORKS

Adams, Virginia M., ed. *On the Altar of Freedom* [diary of James Henry Gooding]. Amherst, Mass., 1991.

Mentions black Confederate sharpshooters in South Carolina (p. 54).

America: Great Crises in our History Told by Its Makers, A Library of Original Sources. Volume III. *The Civil War, 1861-1865.* Chicago, 1925.

Has reference to *Chicago Tribune* article, dated February 20, 1862, which mentions a black who was captured at Fort Donelson, Tenn. (p. 94); also Jeff Davis's coachman (p. 298).

The Civil War Book of Lists. Conshohocken, Penn., 1993.

Six black enlistees; black servants who fought (pp. 169-70); black servant who became Union drummer (p. 182).

Mr. Armistead researches southern history while residing in California.

Bakeless, John. *Spies of The Confederacy.* Philadelphia, 1970.

Black couriers for Belle Boyd (pp 13, 149-50, 162); black spies protected by Sam Davis (pp. 227-28); black servant at Rosser's HQ (p. 38).

Ball, T. H. *A Glance into the Great South-East or, Clarke County, Alabama, and its Surroundings, from 1540 to 1877.* Tuscaloosa, Ala., 1962 [1879].

Black "home guards" (pp. 288-89); drummer Jack Cato (pp. 631-32).

Ballard, Michael B. *A Long Shadow: Jefferson Davis and the Final Days of the Confederacy.* Jackson, Miss., n.d.

Late war movement to arm slaves (pp. 9-13).

Beers, Henry Putney. *Guide to the Archives of the Government of the Confederate States of America.*

Consult categories listed as "Negroes" (p. 93) and "Slaves" (p. 515) for listings of records of black Confederates.

Bennett, Lerone Jr. *Before the Mayflower: A History of the Negro in America, 1619-1964.* Baltimore, 1964.

Mentions the military experiences of the Louisiana Native Guards (p. 169).

Berlin, Ira et al., eds. *Freedom: A Documentary History of Emancipation, 1861-1867. Series II. The Black Military Experience.* Cambridge and New York, 1982.

Contains references to Confederate debate over black enlistment and blacks as military servants (pp. 279-99).

Boddie, William Willis. *History of Williamsburg*. Columbia, S.C., 1923.

Documents the services of servants with Co. I, 4th S.C. Cav., ten of whom received state pensions in 1923 (pp. 355-57); opinions regarding late war legislation to arm slaves (p. 411).

Blackerby, Hubert C. *Blacks in Blue and Gray*: Afro-American Service in the Civil War. Tuscaloosa, Ala., 1979.

Boritt, Gabor S. ed,. *Why the Confederacy Lost*. New York, 1992.

Essay by Joseph T. Glatthaar, "Black Glory: the African-American Role in Union Victory," (pp. 133-62); military labor (pp. 139-40); Louisiana Native Guards (pp. 151-52); General Cleburne's proposal and late war legislation to arm slaves (pp. 159-60).

Botkin, B. A., ed. *A Civil War Treasury of Tales, Legends and Folklore*. New York, 1960.

See the "Planter" incident (pp. 151-53); and more on the Louisiana Native Guards (pp. 153-55).

Bowman, John S., ed. *The Civil War Almanac*. New York, 1983.

Offers references to blacks serving as laborers (p. 68); the "Planter" incident (p. 98); misguiding Dahlgren (p. 186); and late war legislation (pp. 83, 116, 234, 251-52, 255).

Brewer, James H. *The Confederate Negro: Virginia's Craftsmen and Military Laborers, 1861-1865*. Durham, N.C., 1969.

Brown, A. J. *History of Newton County, Mississippi, from 1834 to 1894*. Bowie, Md., 1991 [1894].

Offers evidence of a black fifer for Co. E, 13th Miss. Inf. (p. 81).

Brown, Rita Mae. *High Hearts.*

Foreword mentions 93,000 blacks served in the Confederate Army.

Buchanan, A. Russell. *David S. Terry of California: Dueling Judge.* San Marino, Calif., 1956.

This biography of a prominent California politician who went east to serve as a Confederate officer reports that, during his journey to the Confederacy, he was joined at Monterrey, Mexico, by two free blacks who formerly had been his slaves, but freed when California became a state (1850). They served with him throughout the war (pp. 131-32).

Catton, Bruce. *This Hallowed Ground.* New York, 1961 [1955].

The proposal of General Cleburne and the reaction to it are reported (pp. 378-80); also contains a brief discussion of Confederate governmental activity regarding the recruitment of black soldiers in the last months of the war (pp. 469-70).

____________ and Richard M. Ketchum, eds. *The American Heritage Picture History of the Civil War.* New York, 1960.

Refers to legislation of March 1865 authorizing the formation of black regiments (pp. 509, 591); and Cleburne's proposal (p. 564).

Commager, Henry Steele, ed. *The Blue and the Gray: The Story of the Civil War as Told by Participants.* New York, 1973 [1950].

Provides John Wise's account of VMI black driver at Battle of New Market (Vol. 2: 425).

Cornish, Dudley Taylor. *The Sable Arm: Black Troops in the Union Army, 1861-1865.* Lawrence, Kan., 1987 [1956].

Treats blacks for Confederacy early in war (pp. 7-9); Tennessee's conscription of free blacks (pp. 15-16); Frederick Douglass on blacks in the Confederate army (pp. 16-17); and the Louisiana Native Guards (pp. 66-67).

Cunningham, Frank. *General Stand Watie's Confederate Indians.* San Antonio, 1959.

Reveals blacks in Creek regiment (p. 59); and a number who helped raise money for Confederate war effort (p. 74).

Dabney, Virginius. *The Last Review: The Confederate Reunion, Richmond, 1932.* Chapel Hill, N.C., 1984.

Mentions a black valet of Jefferson Davis (p. 9); contains discussion and photographs of Confederate servant soldiers at reunion (pp. 23, 34, 38-9).

Davis, Burke. *The Long Surrender.* New York, 1985.

Notes March 1865 legislation and enlistment of blacks (pp. 11, 24).

______________. *Our Incredible Civil War.* New York, 1979 [1960].

Discusses VMI driver at Battle of New Market, Va. (p. 37); claims first killing of Union officer by black soldier (p. 13); a black in Jeb Stuart's orchestra (p. 21); bugler at Fredericksburg (p. 49); fighting Atlanta fires, and more on Cleburne's proposal (p 61).

Davis, Jefferson. *The Rise And Fall of the Confederate Government.* New York, 1961 [1889].

Documents acts of February 1864 for black laborers and 1865 legislation and debate (pp. 242-45).

Davis, William C. *Battle At Bull Run: A History of the First Major Campaign of the Civil War.* Garden City, N.Y., 1977.

Reveals that there were blacks who served in Hampton's South Carolina Legion (p. 28) and who constructed earthworks at Manassas (p. 61).

____________. *Breckinridge: Statesman, Soldier, Symbol.* Baton Rouge, La., 1974.

Black Confederates as courier (p. 320); as hospital stewards (p. 366); for non-combat military service (p. 402); plus, Cleburne's proposal (pp 402-3); and the story of Tom Ferguson, servant of General Breckinridge (pp. 524, 528, 537).

____________. *The Orphan Brigade: The Kentucky Confederates Who Couldn't Go Home.* Garden City, N.Y., 1980.

Refers to a black barber of the 4th Kentucky Infantry (p. 246).

Donald, David, ed. *Why the North Won the Civil War.* New York, 1969 [1962].

Indicates that there were black servants who served with the Confederate army (p. 80).

Dowdy, Clifford. *Experiment In Rebellion: The Human Story of the Men Who Guided the Confederacy.* Garden City, N.Y., 1946.

Provides another reference to Cleburne's proposal (p. 368); the 1865 debate on arming slaves (pp. 376, 394); and mentions two uniformed companies of Black Confederates (p. 398).

____________, ed. *The Wartime Papers of R. E. Lee.* New York, 1961.

Contains an 1862 letter regarding the employment of blacks for defense works (p. 99); 1864 letters concerning blacks for defense works (pp. 847-49, 853-54); and an April 1865 letter on detached officers to command black troops (p. 927).

Dufour, Charles L. *Ten Flags in the Wind: The Story of Louisiana.* New York, 1967.

Mentions free blacks who served in Louisiana militia (p. 238).

Durden, Robert F. *The Gray and the Black: The Confederate Debate on Emancipation*. Baton Rouge, La., 1972.

Contains editorials, documents, letters relating to proposals to arm slaves in Confederacy.

Fleming, Walter L. *Civil War and Reconstruction in Alabama*. Gloucester, Mass., 1949 [1905].

See "Negro Troops" (p. 86) and "Negroes During the War" (pp. 205-10).

Foote, Shelby. *The Civil War: A Narrative; Red River to Appomattox*. New York, 1974.

Relates Mary Chesnut's slaves' opinion on being armed for the Confederacy (p. 75); Cleburne's proposal, volunteers at Mobile (pp. 754-55); and the 1865 debate on enlistment (pp. 859-61).

Franklin, John Hope. *From Slavery to Freedom: A History of Negro Americans*. New York, 1967 [1947].

Chronicles the service of blacks as fortification workers (p. 272); in war factories (p. 287); cooks, teamsters, hospital workers (pp. 287-88); Selma arsenal workers (p. 288); as well as more on Cleburne's proposal (p. 289); and the controversial 1865 legislation to arm slaves (p. 289).

Freeman, Douglas Southall. *Lee's Lieutenants*. New York, 1942.

Tom Strother, servant of Richard Taylor, and conversation with Stonewall Jackson (pp. 429-30); "navies" of Capt. C. R. Mason (p. 561).

Fremantle, Arthur J. L. *Three Months in the Southern States, April-June 1863*. Lincoln, Neb., 1991 [1863-64].

A servant named "John" (pp. 68, 76); an oarsman named "Tucker" (p. 97); blacks carrying arms in Alabama (p. 133); a servant named "Aaron" (pp. 148, 172); a black Confederate and his Federal prisoner-of-war (p. 281); slaves as Confederate soldiers (pp. 282, 307).

Gallaway, B. P. *The Ragged Rebel: A Common Soldier in W. H. Parson's Texas Cavalry, 1861-1865.* Austin, 1991 [1988].

Mentions Gen. E. Kirby Smith's September 1864 proposal to arm slaves in Trans-Mississippi West (p. 70).

Glatthaar, Joseph T. *Forged in Battle: The Civil War Alliance of Black Soldiers and White Officers.* New York, 1990.

Discusses reason for free blacks' alignment with Confederacy as addition to strength of Confederacy (pp. 2-4).

Gragg, Rod. *Confederate Goliath: The Battle of Fort Fisher.* New York, 1991.

Impressed slaves work on fort's defenses in North Carolina (pp. 17-18, 60, 100)

Guernsey, Alfred H. and Henry M. Alden. *Harper's Pictorial History of the Civil War.* Chicago, 1866.

Mentions black volunteers, fortification labor, and Louisiana Native Guards (p. 219); and the March 1865 act to arm slaves (p. 753).

Halzsz, Nicholas. *The Rattling Chains: Slave Unrest In The Antebellum South.* New York, 1966.

Louisiana Native Guards (p. 247); servants with Confederate army (p. 250); Cleburne's proposal (p. 251); 1865 legislation to arm slaves (pp. 251-52).

Hargrove, Hondon B. *Black Union Soldiers in the Civil War.* Jefferson, N.C., 1988.

Black volunteers and fortification laborers (pp. 3-4); Tennessee's conscription, Mobile battalion, Cleburne's proposal, debate over arming slaves (pp. 5-6).

Henry, Robert Selph. *The Story of the Confederacy.* New York, 1936.

Cites Cleburne's proposal (p. 379); and debate over arming slaves (pp. 437-40).

Hollandsworth, James G., Jr. *The Louisiana Native Guards: The Black Military Experience During the Civil War*. Baton Rouge, 1995.

First book-length account of this militia unit sanctioned by Louisiana's Confederategovernment.

Horan, James D. *Mathew Brady: Historian With a Camera*. New York, 1955.

One famous photo shows a Confederate lieutenant and his black servant, both of whom captured by Custer (p. 152).

Hurst, Jack. *Nathan Bedford Forrest: A Biography*. New York, 1993.

Cleburne's proposal (p. 160); March 1865 legislation to arm slaves (p. 254).

Jones, John B. *A Rebel War Clerk's Diary*. New York, 1958.

Mentions blacks as fortification laborers (pp. 377, 417); debate over arming slaves (pp. 457, 459, 495, 496, 499-501, 503-5, 507, 513, 518); parade of black troops in Richmond (pp. 521, 522); recruitment of blacks (pp. 524, 525).

Jones, Katharine M., ed. *Heroines of Dixie: Winter of Desperation*. New York,1975 [1955].

Reports the war from May 1863 until its close through excerpts from diaries and letters of southern women. Sara Rice Pryor provides an account of "John," a black servant, who accompanied her husband, Gen. Roger A. Pryor, throughout the war (p. 62).

Jordan, Ervin L., Jr. *Black Confederates and Afro-Yankees in Civil War Virginia*. Charlottesville, Va., 1995.

Keller, Allan. *Morgan's Raid*. Indianapolis, 1961.

Morgan's servant, Box, harassing Union prisoners and escaping back to the Confederacy (pp. 44, 185-87).

Krick, Robert K. *The Fredericksburg Artillery.* Lynchburg, Va., 1986.

Two Virginia blacks enlist and serve with this unit as soldiers (pp. 71, 103).

Lattimore, Ralston B. *Fort Pulaski National Monument.* Washington, D.C., 1961 [1954].

Depicts blacks digging mud from moat (p. 15); and Blind Tom raising funds for the Confederate war effort in Savannah (p. 31).

Lee, Fitzhugh. *General Lee.* Greenwich, Conn., 1961 [1893].

Mentions servants with South Carolina troops (p. 109); their help in deceiving McClellan during the Peninsula Campaign (p. 164); Lee's steward, Bryan (pp. 223-24); and General Lee's support of the arming of slaves (p. 350).

*Little, George and James R. Maxwell. *A History of Lumsden's Battery C. S. A.* Tuscaloosa, Ala., 1988 [1905].

Features blacks in a reunion photo; Jim Bobbett, on the duties of servants in the army (p. 19); blacks as cooks (p. 24); as foragers (p. 51); Jim Bobbett's activities, loyalty of servants (pp. 60-61); foraging incident (p. 62).

Long, E. B. and Barbara Long. *The Civil War Day By Day.* Garden City, N.Y., 1971.

Notes February 1864 act for black laborers and March 1865 act to arm slaves (p. 708).

Longstreet, James A. *From Manassas to Appomattox: Memoirs of the Civil War in America.* New York, 1991 [1895].

Refers to a black servant guiding General J.E.B. Stuart about Pope's headquarters (p. 165:); a black Confederate and his Federal p.o.w. on the retreat from Gettysburg (pp. 427-28); and offers an opinion regarding officers for black troops (p. 651).

---

* See selection reprinted above, pp. 151-52.

Massey, John. *Reminiscences Giving Sketches of Scenes through which the Author has Passed and Pen Portraits of People who have Modified his Life*. Nashville, 1916.

Mentions a black fifer and drummer of the University of Alabama Corps of Cadets (p. 138); and Lem, servant of Orderly Sergeant Micou of 1st Battalion Infantry, Hilliard's Alabama Legion (pp. 167, 172-73).

McMichael, Lois. *History of Butts County, Georgia, 1825-1976*. Easley, S.C., 1988.

Notes that blacks help to bury dead after Battle of Sunshine Church (p. 440).

McPherson, James M. *Marching Toward Freedom: Blacks in the Civil War, 1861-1865*. New York, 1991 [1965].

Documents a black southerner's account of serving Confederate artillery pieces at First Manassas (pp. 34, 36-38); reproduces photo of a black in a Confederate camp (p. 35); discusses debate over the arming of slaves (pp. 38-39).

Monaghan, Jay. *Civil War on the Western Border: 1854-1865*. Boston, 1955.

Provides references to a servant of Gen. Albert Pike (p. 234); blacks in a Creek Indian Regiment (p. 235); and their participation in the Battle of Pea Ridge (p. 241).

Monroe County Historical Society. *Monroe County, Georgia: A History*. Forsyth, Ga., 1979.

Black servants and laborers help to build hospital accomodations (pp. 153-54).

Mullen, Robert. *Blacks in America's Wars*. New York, 1973.

More about the Louisiana Native Guards (pp. 22-23, 31).

Nichols, G. W. *A Soldier's Story of His Regiment and Incidentally of the Lawton-Gordon-Evans Brigade, Army Northern Virginia.* Kennesaw, Ga., 1961 [1898].

A private in the 61st Georgia Infantry recalls black Confederates twice in passing and relates one incident of note. Black cooks at Confederate military hospitals are cited (p. 70); as well as how "Rube," a servant of a lieutenant of the regiment, retrieved his wounded master from the field. In the context of a joke played on one officer, his black cook is also mentioned (p. 132).

*Oates, William C. *The War Between the Union and the Confederacy and its Lost Opportunities. . . .* New York, 1905.

Osborne, Charles C. *Jubal: The Life and Times of General Jubal A. Early, CSA, Defender of the Lost Cause.* Chapel Hill, 1992.

Details Early's objection to black militia participation in 1875 Stonewall Jackson monument parade and black servants of Stonewall Brigade who marched in the parade along with white veterans (pp. 418-19).

Parish, Peter J. *The American Civil War.* New York, 1975.

Mentions the services of blacks as military laborers (pp. 326-27).

Parks, Joseph H. *General Leonidas Polk, C. S. A.: The Fighting Bishop.* Baton Rouge, 1990 [1962].

Refers to Polk's servant, Altimore (pp. 278, 384).

Pendleton, Louis. *Alexander H. Stephens.* Philadelphia, 1907.

Includes debate over arming slaves and information on a black battalion at Mobile (pp. 270-72).

---

*See selection reprinted above, pp. 148-50.

Peters, James Edward. *Arlington National Cemetery: Shrine to America's Heroes*. 1986.

Notes that blacks were deliberately included on the Confederate Monument (p. 253).

Picture It: The Civil War. Jackson, Miss., n.d.

Summary of Civil War events and sites in Mississippi refers to black Confederates twice: a monument at Canton honoring freed slaves who served (p. 10); and former slaves who fought for the Confederacy were admitted as inmates to the Jeff Davis Confederate Soldiers' Home at Beauvoir (p. 19).

Pollard, Edward A. *Southern History of the War*. 1977 [1866].

Contains debate over arming slaves and references to black companies drilling in Richmond (pp. 471-73).

Quarles, Benjamin. *The Negro in the Civil War*. Boston, 1969 [1953].

Treats the black experience on both sides during the war, including black Confederates who were servants often under fire (p. iv); volunteered for the war effort (pp. 35-38); impressed for military and fortification labor (pp. 47-48, 215, 273-81); contraband (pp. 58-60); as well as the question of black loyalty (pp. 49-50, 263-67); a servant with the 6th Alabama (pp. 62-63); the "Planter" incident (pp. 71-73); Pemberton's black spy (pp. 87-88); the Louisiana Native Guards (pp. 116-17); Cleburne's proposal (pp. 276-77); and the debate over arming slaves and the recruitment of blacks (pp. 278-81).

Riffel, Judy, ed. *A History of Pointe Coupee Parish and its Families*. Baton Rouge, 1983.

Mentions a free black militia company (pp. 49-50).

Rollins, Richard, ed. *Black Southerners in Gray: Essays on Afro-Americans in Confederate Armies*. Murfreesboro, Tenn., 1994.

Russell, Charles Wells, ed. *Gray Ghost: The Memoirs of Colonel John S. Mosby.* New York, 1992 [1917].

Mentions Mosby's servant, Aaron (pp. 71, 113); and a servant in the headquarters of J.E.B. Stuart (pp. 77-78).

Saunders, James Edmonds. *Early Settlers of Alabama.* Baltimore, 1982 [1899].

The Governor of Alabama appointed Saunders aide-de-camp to raise blacks for defense work (p. 17); also mentions a servant of Col. Jesse Forrest (p. 28).

Shenkman, Richard and Kurt Reiger. *One-Night Stands with American History: Odd, Amusing, and Little-Known Incidents.* New York, 1982.

Contends that there were more than 93,000 black Confederate soldiers (p. 106).

Smith, Page. *Trial By Fire: A People's History of the Civil War and Reconstruction.* New York, 1982.

Contains synopsis of Cleburne's proposal, servants who accompanied their masters to war, an example of a black sharpshooter, and late war debate over formal arming of slaves for Confederate service (pp. 329-30).

Sons of Confederate Veterans Ancestor Album. Houston, 1986.

Mentions activities of black servants with masters in Confederate units (pp. 35, 46, 56, 57, 59, 77, 121, 137, 144, 166, 171, 177, 187, 218); photograph of uniformed black Confederate (p. 187).

Sorrel, G. Moxley. *Recollections of a Confederate Staff Officer.* New York, 1992 [1905].

Refers to servant of a colonel of the 19th Mississippi Infantry (p. 41); servants of other officers (p. 99); and Sorrel's own servant at Petersburg (pp. 237-38).

Stern, Philip Van Doren. *The Confederate Navy: A Pictorial History*. Garden City, NY, 1962.

Notes the "Planter" incident (p. 111).

____________ ed. *Soldier Life in the Union and Confederate Armies*. Greenwich, Conn., 1961.

Documents duties of blacks, their contribution to Confederate morale (pp. 294-95); as company servants (p. 298).

Sulzby, James F. Jr. *Toward a History of Samford University*. 2 Vols. Birmingham, 1986.

Cites a black, female nurse at Howard College Military Hospital, Marion, Ala. (1: 52).

Symonds, Craig L. *Joseph E. Johnston: A Civil War Biography*. New York, 1992.

Blacks as replacement for whites in non-combatant military roles (p. 260); Cleburne's proposal (pp. 251, 260-61).

Taylor, Richard. *Destruction and Reconstruction: Personal Experiences of the Late War*. New York, 1992 [1879].

Contains various references to the role of black Confederates, including: marching order of servants with army (p. 64); Taylor's own servant, Tom Strother (pp. 65-68, 72, 87, 90, 233, 270); military labor of blacks (pp. 129, 140-41); black POWs who volunteer to fight for the Confederacy (p. 249); and railroad laborers (pp. 260, 266).

Thomas, Emory M. *The Confederate Nation, 1861-1865*. New York, 1979.

Discusses Cleburne's proposal (pp. 261-64); Jefferson Davis's opnion on arming slaves (pp. 290-94); the March 1865 legislation to arm slaves (pp. 295-97); the legislation authorizing employment in non-combat military occupations (p. 260);

and includes an extensive bibliography on blacks in the Confederacy (pp. 358-60).

____________. *The Confederate State of Richmond: A Biography of the Capital.* Austin and London, 1971.

Briefly discusses wartime service of blacks to the Confederacy, the debate over arming slaves, and black soldiers drilling in Richmond's Capitol Square (pp. 189-90).

Trask, Benjamin. *16th Virginia Infantry.* Lynchburg, Va., 1986.

Blacks armed for the Confederacy (p. 28).

Vandiver, Frank E. *Mighty Stonewall.* College Station, Tex., 1974 [1957].

See Capt. C.R. Mason and his black laborers (p. 311).

____________. *Their Tattered Flags: The Epic of the Confederacy.* New York, 1970.

Early debate on arming slaves (p. 284).

Ward, Geoffrey C. *The Civil War: An Illustrated History.* New York, 1990.

Gen. R. E. Lee's opinion on arming slaves, as well as two companies of black hospital orderlies (p. 363).

Watkins, Sam R. *Co. Aytch.* New York, 1962 [1885].

Comments on servants after the battle of Shiloh (p. 43); Gen. Braxton Bragg's attitude toward blacks (p. 48); the cook of a colonel of the 1st Tennessee Infantry (p. 92); and Gen. Joseph E. Johnston's treatment of black Confederates (p. 127).

Wiley, Bell Irvin. *Embattled Confederates: An Illustrated History of Southerners at War*. New York, 1964.

Duties of blacks as servants and in battle (pp. 234-35); fortification labor photo (p. 236); mule drive photo (p. 238); debate over arming of slaves (241-44).

____________. *The Life of Johnny Reb: The Common Soldier of the Confederacy*. Baton Rouge, 1992 [1943].

Presents black Confederates involved in a snowball fight (p. 65); as servants (p. 99); as cooks (pp. 103-4); doing laundry (p. 107); as informal mail carriers for soldiers (pp. 150, 199-200); as well as duties and activities as servants, as fortification laborers, and the debate over arming slaves (pp. 327-30).

____________. *Southern Negroes, 1861-1865*. New Haven, Conn., 1938.

Williams, George W. *A History of the Negro Troops in the War of the Rebellion, 1864-1865*. n.p., 1888.

*Wilson, Joseph T. *The Black Phalanx: A History of the Negro Soldiers of the United States, 1775-1865*. Hartford, Conn., 1890.

Winters, John D. *The Civil War in Louisiana*. Baton Rouge, 1985 [1963].

Treats free Negro local-protection companies (p. 31); free black militia and their reasons for fighting (p. 34); Louisiana Native Guards (p. 35); monetary contributions to war effort (p. 39); as fortification labor (pp. 223, 246); and the Governor's support for the arming of slaves (p. 383).

Woodward, C. Vann, ed. *Mary Chesnut's Civil War*. New Haven, Conn., 1981.

Mrs. Chestnut records opinions, white and black, on the arming of slaves (pp. 255-56, 313, 545, 678-79).

---

*See selection reprinted above, pp. 144-46.

Woodworth, Steven E. *Jefferson Davis and His Generals: The Failure of Confederate Command in the West.* Lawrence, Kan., 1990.

Cleburne's proposal (pp. 262-63).

Worsham, John H. *One of Jackson's Foot Cavalry: His Experiences and What He Saw During the War 1861-1865.* New York, 1992 [1912].

Black cooks involved in battle, white troops caring for a servants who's ill (pp. 175-76).

Wyeth, John Allan. *That Devil Forrest: Life of General Nathan Bedford Forrest.* Baton Rouge, La., 1989 [1899].

Notes when Forrest frees his black teamsters (pp. xxi, 546); and when a teamster drowns while on campaign (p. 262).

Young, J. P. *The Seventh Tennessee Cavalry: A History.*

List the names of 38 "colored men" in Companies E and L.

SCHOLARLY ARTICLES

Berry, Mary F., "Negro Troops in Blue and Gray: the Louisiana Native Guards, 1861-1863" *Louisiana History* 8 (1967): 165-90.

Dibble, Ernest F., "Slave Rentals to the Military, Pensacola and the Gulf Coast" *Civil War History* 23 (1977): 101-13.

Dillard, Philip D., "The Confederate Debate Over Arming Slaves: Views from Macon and Augusta Newspapers" *Georgia Historical Quarterly* 79 (1995): 117-46.

Escott, Paul D., "The Context of Freedom: Georgia's Slaves During the Civil War" *Georgia Historical Quarterly* 53 (1974): 79-104.

Hay, Thomas R., "The South and the Arming of the Slaves" *Mississippi Valley Historical Review* 7 (1919): 34-73.

Mohr, Clarence L., "Southern Blacks in the Civil War: a Century of Historiography" *Journal of Negro History* 69 (1974): 174-95.

Nelson, Bernard H., "Some Aspects of Negro Life in North Carolina During the Civil War" *North Carolina Historical Review* 25 (1948): 143-66.

Reid, Bill C., "Confederate Opponents of Arming the Slaves" *Journal of Mississippi History* 22 (1960): 249-70.

Reid, Robert D., "The Negro in Alabama During the Civil War" *Journal of Negro History* 35 (1950): 265-88.

Spraggins, Tinsley L., "Mobilization of Negro Labor for the Department of Virginia and North Carolina, 1861-1865" *Journal of Negro History* 31 (1946): 392-410.

Stephenson, Nathaniel W., "The Question of Arming the Slaves" *American Historical Review* 18 (1913): 295-308.

Trexler, Harrison A., "The Opposition of Planters to Employment of Slaves as Laborers by the Confederacy" *Mississippi Valley Historical Review* 27 (1940): 211-24.

Wesley, Charles H., "The Employment of Negroes in the Confederate Army" *Journal of Negro History* 4 (1919): 239-53.

MAGAZINE ARTICLES

Carroll, Jeff, "Dignity, Courage and Fidelity" *Confederate Veteran* (Nov.-Dec. 1990).

Frimus Kelly, servant with the 8th Texas Cavalry (pp. 26-27).

Lunsford, P. Charles, "The Forgotten Confederates" *Confederate Veteran* (Nov.-Dec. 1992).

Bill Yopp and Amos Rucker, Georgia Black Confederates (pp. 12-15).

____________, "Attacks on the Colors, Arguments Against Confederate Symbols" *Confederate Veteran* (Jan.-Feb. 1994).

Proposed memorial to black Confederates at Nottoway County, Va. (pp. 4-6).

Mancini, John, "Fantastic Voyage: The Long Raid of the C.S.S. Shenandoah" *Civil War: The Magazine of the Civil War Society* 11 (Jul.-Aug. 1993).

Mentions two American blacks among crew (p. 10).

Mitchell, Joseph B., "Attacks on the Colors: Ken Burns--One Year Later" *Confederate Veteran* (Mar.-Apr. 1992): 4-10.

Obatala, J. K., "The Unlikely Story of Blacks Who Were Loyal to Dixie" *Smithsonian Magazine* 9 (March 1979): 94-101.

Smith, Edward C., "Calico, Black and Gray: Women and Blacks in the Confederacy" *Civil War: The Magazine of the Civil War Society.*

__________, "New South" *Civil War: The Magazine of the Civil War Society* 10 (Nov.-Dec. 1992).

Steger, Wallace, "Our Saddest War" *Coronet Magazine* (April 1961).

Treats blacks as servants and as teamsters, and armed in March 1865 (p. 67).

Tyler, Greg, "Rebel Drummer Henry Brown" *Civil War Times Illustrated* 27 (Feb. 1989).

Free black drummer of the 8th South Carolina Infantry (pp. 22-23).

Young, Mel, "The Great Gettysburg Robbery--Who Stole the Commissary Funds?" *Confederate Veteran* (Mar.-Apr. 1994).

SLAVE NARRATIVES

During the 1930s, the Federal Writers' Project hired unemployed writers and researchers to interview and to record the oral histories of former slaves. The interviews were typed and stored in the Library of Congress under the title "Slave Narratives: A Folk History of Slavery in the U. S. from Interviews With Former Slaves." These oral histories by former slaves are extremely interesting in themselves, enlightening and even, at times, surprising. Some of the former slaves interviewed spoke of their own experience in the Confederate army, and others recalled service by relatives or other slaves on the same plantation. The slave narratives have been made available to the general public in:

Botkin, Benjamin A. *Lay My Burden Down: A Folk History of Slavery*. Chicago, 1965.

Hurmence, Belinda, ed. *Before Freedom: 48 Oral Histories of Former North and South Carolina Slaves*. New York, 1990.

ACKNOWLEDGMENTS

The invaluable contributions of a large number of individuals and organizations have made this volume possible. We are indebted to the late Prof. C. W. Harper of North Carolina State University, Prof. Jay S. Hoar of the University of Maine at Farmington, Dr. Erving L. Jordan, Jr., of the University of Virginia, and Dr. John McGlone, editor/publisher of *The Journal of Confederate History*. We appreciate the counsel of Gene C. Armistead, Thomas Spratt, Dr. Wayne Austerman, James West Thompson, the Rev. Edward Raffetto, and Jim Vogler, editor of *The Confederate Veteran*. In addition, the readership of the *Veteran* provided significant archival findings and, although space limitations prevented many of these items from being printed, we would like to identify these contributors, and have attempted to do so, in a listing at the end of this volume. For those we have omitted, please forgive us. There is an abundance of material still awaiting publication.

Special thanks to Arthur Shilstone, illustrator for *Smithsonian* and *Life* magazines; to Monty Hudson, archival photographer and southern scholar; and to Gail DeLoach, photograph specialist with the Georgia Department of Archives and History, Atlanta. Production assistance was provided by Diane Daniel, Linda Wilkins Murphy, Marie H. Segars, as well as by Dr. James Burney and Mrs. Michele Walker, of the Educational Computing Lab at the University of North Alabama, Florence. And we appreciate the material submitted from a host of historical societies, in particular: the Darlington (South Carolina) Historical Commission; the Historical Center of York County (South Carolina) and the Wake County (North Carolina) Genealogical Society. Also we wish to thank the research personnel at the following libraries: National Archives; Library of Congress; Museum of the Confederacy at Richmond; the William Pullen Library of Georgia State University; the Robert W. Woodruff Library of Emory University; Special Collections, The University of Tennessee, Knoxville; and the Departments of Archives and History in the states of Georgia, South Carolina, and Tennessee.

Special acknowledgment is made by the editors to Mr. and Mrs. E. V. Barrow, Mr. and Mrs George F. Fleming, James and India Barrow, and to Lynn and Jonathan, Joel, and J. Leigh. May we never forget the story of all the peoples of the Confederacy, and the extraordinary vision of Gen. Pat Cleburne. And may we each serve an Almighty God, as taught in *Matthew* 22: 37-40.

CONTRIBUTORS

(ALABAMA): Leonard Wilson; Richard A. Kelly; Eddie Smith; C. Hodo Strickland; Billy E. Price; James Shannon Hunter; Charles M. Simon; Elliott R. Matthews; David R. Center; Roy E. Smith; Lewis D. Brasell; Richard Jesse; Kenneth Lee Brown; Greg Swanner; Menzo W. Driskell, Jr.

(ARKANSAS): William A. Myers; Edwin Lee Chaney; J. G. Tarbell.

(CALIFORNIA): Stephen R. Renouf; Richard M. Rollins; Jim Guild; Ronnie V. Gregory; K. Davidson; Randy "Virgil" Burroughs; Gene C. Armistead; Larry W. Carder; Dr. Phillip Thomas Tucker; Brock Townsend.

(CANADA): Scott Baylay.

(FLORIDA): Col. Grover Criswell; Henry V. McCrea; Arthur J. Chesser; Hewitt J. DuPont; Robert Mann; Linton E. Floyd, III; Mr. & Mrs. J. R. Armitage; J. C. Robertson; James L. Harrison; Bill Maxwell; Dr. Richard Lancaster; Paul C. Pace.

(GEORGIA): John & Kay Black of All Medica, Inc.; Walter S. McCleskey; Keith D. Beck; John Wayne Dobson; Kim S. Hendren; T. Wayne Marshall; Thomas E. Lyle; O. Houston Endsley, Jr.; Greg White; Hugh W. Barrow; P. Charles Lunsford; Emory Lavender, *The Countryman Newspaper*; Miss Sandra Fields; Dietrich W. Oellerich, Jr.; Scott K. Gilbert, Jr.; Gen. Patrick R. Cleburne Camp #1361, S.C.V.; Gen. John B. Gordon Memorial Camp #1449, S.C.V.; James M. Gaston, Jr.; Rev. & Mrs. William D. Buckalew, Jr.; James L. Lester, Jr.; A. O. Smith; Pat C. Cates; Ken Smith.

(HAWAII): Rev. Dr. Robert O. Neff.

(INDIANA): Stephen L. Ritchie.

(KANSAS): Jess Estes.

(KENTUCKY): Lon Carter Barton; John Britton Wells, III; J. Andrew White; Albert L. Page; Stephen L. King; Kenneth C. Thomson.

(LOUISIANA): Keith A. Roy, Jr.; Alvin Y. Brethard; Eric J. Brock.
(MAINE): Jay S. Hoar.

(MARYLAND): Robert A. Crawley; Mr. J. Couch; James S. Clark.

(MICHIGAN): Geoff Walden; Stephen D. Lutz.

(MISSISSIPPI): Thomas S. McCaskey; Rev. Gale Anderson; Dan Estes; Bobby Mitchell; Kerry Gregory; Alan Whitehead; Linn Hart; Paul C. Cartwright; Charles Smith Wilburn.

(MISSOURI): Kevin Tilly; Gary Parkin; Harold Dellinger; Marshall H. Ruxton; Francis Chandler Furman; Bill & Ellie Bowden; Richard Alan Young.

(NEW JERSEY): George W. Wright.

(NEW YORK): Albert L. Sheppard; Steven R. Teeft; Khalid Hashim Bey; John T. Histed; H. Gerald Starnes.

(NORTH CAROLINA): Terry Crayton; Thomas W. Shaver; Scott T. Glass; Pete Peters; Tom Alderson; Hunter Edwards; James Alfred Locke Miller; Philip Sloan; Walter E. Bigger, Jr.; Rev. Troy Wiley; Miss Bess R. Hubbard; Rudolph Young.

(NORWAY): Lars Gjertveit.

(OKLAHOMA): Terry W. Hall; Les R. Tucker; Joe S. Hays.

(PENNSYLVANIA): Ronald Lee Glazier.

(SOUTH CAROLINA): Walter Brian Cisco; Miss Vickie C. Tompkins; Brett Bradshaw; Allan Thigpen; Mark L. Watts; Mr. & Mrs. W. C. Smith, III; Wayne D. Carroll; Charles E. Park, President, The Confederate States of America, Historical Preservation Society; Glenda Bundrick; Max Dorsey; Tommie J. Vaughan; Robert N. Rosen.

(SOUTH DAKOTA): James A. Gabel.

(SWEDEN): Thomas Johnsson, President, Confederate States Allied-Europe.

(TENNESSEE): Steven R. Jones; Miss Marcia Abernathy; Ronald T. Clemmons; Walter L. Bates; Stewart Cruickshunk; Daniel Gregory; Ridly Wills, II; William E. Griffis, Jr.; Tim Burgess; Dr. Robert S. Dotson; Ronny Mangrum; John D. Boniol; Jim Balloch; Malcolm H. Liles.

(TEXAS): James N. Vogler, Jr.; William Hadskey; Daniel J. Hayes; Maj. Warner D. Farr; Wilbur Thomas Myers; Cherry Gaffney; John Carr; Bruce & Ann Marshall; Mrs. June E. Tuck; Ben S. Grimland; C. E. Avery; Mark Farrington; Mr. & Mrs. Timothy D. Hudson; Bruce Williford; Confederate Calendar Works; Carl Hill; Bruce Cunningham; James Cunningham; Norman D. Brown; Reynolds M. Cushman; Mrs. Marian Minniece; William O. Grimes; Scott Buie.

(UNITED KINGDOM): Maurice Rigby; David Key Canfil.

(VIRGINIA): Edward S. Milligan; Thomas M. Spratt; William F. Hinson, Jr.; Harry L. Jackson; Mrs. John Board; Miss Patricia Buck; Blane L. Zirilli; Col. J. A. Barton Campbell; William B. Mixon, Jr.; Maurice L. Lucas; Dorsey A. Howard; Lewis Leigh, Jr.

(WEST VIRGINIA): Jack L. Dickinson; Dr. Gerald T. Golden.

THE EDITORS

Charles Kelly Barrow, a native of Georgia, former legislative aide to the Georgia General Assembly, and a historical researcher, is employed in the cotton industry. A graduate of Shorter College, he is also Historian of the Georgia Division, Sons of Confederate Veterans.

J. H. Segars, an administrator with the Georgia Department of Education in Atlanta, is author of *In Search of Confederate Ancestors* and editor of *Andersonville: The Southern Perspective.*

Dr. R. B. Rosenburg, Assistant Professor of History at the University of North Alabama, formerly served on the editorial staff of *The Papers of Andrew Johnson* and as managing editor of *The Journal of East Tennessee History*. His publications include *Living Monuments: Confederate Soldiers' Homes in the New South.*

INDEX

The Journal of Confederate History Book Series

Published by Southern Heritage Press

The Journal of Confederate History Book Series, founded by Dr. John McGlone in Murfreesboro, Tennessee, is primarily sold through national historic site book stores, small independent book sellers, national Civil War publication mail order and individual subcriptions.

A partial list of subscribers include University libraries at the U. S. Military Academy, Southwest Missouri State, Rice, Boston College, Cornell, Texas, Duke, Elon College, Harvard, Florida State, Illinois, Texas Christian, Penn State, Marquette, Memphis, Auburn, Southeasten Louisiana, Winthrop, Tulane, Yale, California, Texas A&M, Western Ontario, Georgia, Central Oklahoma, and the Virginia Military Institute.

Eastern National Book Stores sell the Journal of Confederate History Book Series at the following historic sites: Gettysburg, Wilson's Creek, Fredericksburg, Andersonville, Atlanta Cyclorama, Natchez Trace Parkway, Chickamauga & Chattanooga, Vicksburg, Stones River, and Shiloh.

THESE VOLUMES OF THE JOURNAL OF CONFEDERATE HISTORY BOOK SERIES ARE STILL AVAILABLE IN LIMITED QUANTITIES:

Vol. 8 *For the Sake of My Country: the Diary of Col. W. W. Ward.* R. B. Rosenburg, editor. $12.00
Vol. 9 *In Search of Confederate Ancestors: The Guide*, J.H. Segars. $10.00
Vol. 10 *A Nation of Sovereign States*, Archie McDonald, editor. $12.00
Vol. 12 *They Sleep Beneath the Mockingbird* by Harold Cross. $12.00
Vol. 13 *Andersonville: The Southern Perspective*, J. H. Segars, editor. $15.00
Vol. 14 *Forgotten Confederates: An Anthology About Black Southerners*, Barrow, et al. $15.00

To order: send check or money order to:
Southern Heritage Press
Circulation Dept.
Post Office Box 347163
Atlanta, Georgia 30334

A NOTE TO OUR SUBSCRIBERS

In order to better serve those of you who make our publication possible, we are changing the way we handle subscriptions. Instead of offering a four issue subscription that takes two years to fulfill, we now offer each new volume to our regular (and new) subscribers on a single issue basis. When your current subscription expires, you may continue to receive each new issue of the *Journal of Confederate History* Book Series by sending $15.00 check or money order to Southern Heritage Press, Post Office Box 347163, Atlanta, GA 30334.

Southern Heritage Press will continue to publish two volumes of this series each year and number them in sequence as in the past. Volumes I - VII are no longer in print and are considered by some book dealers to be collectibles. Museums, universities, libraries, and other institutions may continue to subscribe on the four book plan for $43.95 per subscription, if they wish.

We hope that the changes will be more beneficial to our regular subscribers. Remember, we will still notify you of upcoming titles when your receive each current issue. Every effort will be made in continuing to bring you the "best in Confederate history" and we welcome your comments, suggestions, and manuscript proposals. For those interested in financially supporting the journal through charter subscribtions, or in advertising through our ad pages, please write us for details and rates.

Thank you for your continued support and encouragement.

THE COURIER

Civil War Newspaper

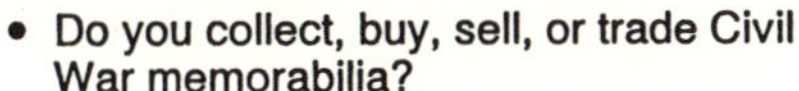

- Do you collect, buy, sell, or trade Civil War memorabilia?
- Are you searching for specific information relating to a certain battle, prison, ship, regiment, or individual who fought in the Civil War?
- Do you provide goods/services for Civil War buffs?
- Are you recruiting members for a CWRT, SCV, SUV, Reenactment or Skirmish organization, or similar group of buffs?

IF SO, **THE COURIER** WILL HELP YOU!

SEND FOR A **FREE** SAMPLE COPY TODAY!

(Please allow up to 4-5 weeks for delivery)

---------------------- clip here ----------------------

Yes, I'd like to receive a free copy of **THE COURIER.**
Please send it to: *(Please print)*

NAME: ______________________________

ADDRESS: ______________________________

CITY: ______________________________

STATE: ______________ ZIP: ______________

PLEASE CHECK ONE:

_______ Reenactor

_______ Skirmisher

_______ SUV

_______ SCV

_______ CWRT

_______ Other

THE COURIER

2503 Delaware Ave. • Buffalo, New York 14216
Phone (716) 873-2594 • FAX (716) 873-0809

THE CONFEDERATE VETERAN